Small Appliance Repair

BY BYRON WELS

GROSSET
GOOD LIFE
BOOKS

PUBLISHERS • GROSSET & DUNLAP • NEW YORK

A FILMWAYS COMPANY

Acknowledgments

The author would especially like to thank the General Electric Corporation and Sears, Roebuck and Co., whose cooperation made work on this book a great deal easier.

For Susan, Happicairn and Bethlehem.

Copyright © 1977 by Grosset & Dunlap, Inc.
All rights reserved
Published simultaneously in Canada
Library of Congress catalog card number: 76-571
ISBN 0-448-12286-3 (trade edition)
ISBN 0-448-13372-5 (library edition)
First printing 1977
Printed in the United States of America

Contents

1. Why Not Repair It Yourself? 5
2. Safety First 8
3. Tools You'll Need 11
4. Fault Analysis 14
5. Electric Motors in General 16
6. Electric Toasters 19
7. Toaster Ovens 21
8. Electric Clocks 23
9. Electric Carving Knives 26
10. Meat Slicers 28
11. Vibrators 30
12. Vacuum Cleaners 32
13. Blenders 35
14. Electric Shavers 40
15. Air Fresheners and Humidifiers 42
16. Electric Blankets 45
17. Electric Pencil Sharpeners 47
18. Phonographs/Stereos 49
19. Electric Lamps 51
20. Hair Dryers 54
21. Electric Heaters 56
22. Electric Mixers 57
23. Telephone Answering Machines 61
24. Electric Irons 63
25. Electric Fans 65
26. Cassette Players and Recorders 68
27. Electric Knife Sharpeners 70
28. Electric Can Openers 72
29. Malted Milk Machines 75
    Fault-Analysis Chart 76
    Index 80

1
Why Not Repair It Yourself?

A small appliance is one of many devices that can make life easier and more pleasant. Like most modern contrivances, however, the small appliance is not built to last forever. In time, even the best small appliance will exhibit signs that tell you something is wrong with it. When this happens, you turn it off, pull out the plug, and glare at the unit. You've got a decision to make. Should you throw it away and buy a new one? Should you take it to the local repair shop for an overhaul? Or — and this is what this book is all about — should you try to repair it yourself?

Our own feeling is that before you junk the unit, rush it to an expensive repairman, or go out and spend your hard-earned money on a new one, you should try to repair the appliance yourself. If you do repair it yourself, you will save some money and will experience the pride of accomplishment in completing such a job.

But other considerations may negate this argument. Some electric can openers can be bought for less than five dollars. Does it really pay to repair such a unit when the cost of a replacement is that low? From a financial point of view, perhaps it doesn't, but the satisfaction you get repairing the unit is worth more than the five dollars. In that way, it pays, and pays well.

Another consideration, of course, is the manufacturer's warranty.

If a unit fails while still under warranty, by all means take advantage of it and have the manufacturer repair or replace the unit. But if you try to repair an appliance that is under warranty and find you can't, the manufacturer may not accept the appliance for servicing or replacement. Most manufacturers "seal" the units, either with a paper patch over one of the dismounting nuts, or a small spot of paint over the nut. If the patch or paint has been disturbed (as it would have to be if you had opened it), the unit's warranty is voided.

So we're going to be dealing with appliances that fail after the warranty has run out, and that offer you only the options of either the local repairman or your own ministrations.

First, let's set a few things straight. You don't have to be an electrical engineer to repair an appliance, and you do not need an in-depth knowledge of electricity. You won't require an elaborate set of tools and your kitchen table will do nicely as a work bench.

You *can* effect excellent repairs by following the procedures in this book.

What you need is a bit of detecting ability to find out what went wrong and a few skills required to change a bad part for a good part. That's really all it takes. Your electrical appliance worked once. A part went bad. Now your job is to locate the part that went bad and replace it with a good part. Having done so, the unit should work again. Okay, that's a simple explanation. Sometimes a part goes bad and triggers a chain of events that ends with blowing out a fuse. One part goes bad, causing another part to fail, and then another to malfunction. Your detective work requires that you follow the chain of events to the bitter end. But, with patience, you can locate the ultimate fault, follow the chain back, and make a repair.

Never overlook the obvious. We have seen repairmen take an entire unit apart on the word of the customer that "It just quit working." "Did the motor run?" asks the repairman. "No," replies the customer. What had actually happened? The customer's wife knocked out the wall plug with her vacuum cleaner and forgot to plug it in again. People forget about such things, because some appliances are always left connected. Never assume anything, and always make suitable tests yourself.

Many times, an appliance will be self-analyzing, if you know what to look for.

For example, if the motor of a rotisserie works but the unit doesn't heat, this would indicate that there is a fault in one or more of the heating elements or in the circuits that control the heating elements.

If a vacuum cleaner does not pick up dirt, but the motor operates, you can assume that there's a problem in the vacuum system — perhaps a bag that needs changing, or possibly a blockage of the hose. The observation that "The vacuum cleaner doesn't work" is not sufficient in diagnosing a problem.

A physician uses more than one diagnostic device before he renders an opinion. He takes your temperature to determine if you have a fever, checks your pulse, respiration, and heart, and tests your blood pressure. Then, only after making several tests, does he render an opinion and recommend treatment.

You cannot look at a unit in a superficial manner and begin the repairs. You have to proceed slowly, taking every possibility into consideration, and only then reach a decision and take a course of action.

How you make those repairs is equally important. If you have correctly diagnosed a malfunction, properly selected a course of action, and then make a slapdash repair, you're soon going to be in trouble with that unit again. You are within bounds to make a hasty repair just to test your own judgment — but the hasty repair will not and cannot last, and should be reworked properly once you have established that this is where the fault lies.

Suppose you have an electric toaster that works, but always leaves one side of a slice of bread untoasted. You disassemble the unit and find that there's a break in the circuit of one of the heater elements. You bridge this break by twisting a piece of wire from one side of the break to the other, reassemble the toaster, and try it out. Eureka! It works. If you now return the toaster to service, it will only be a matter of time before it's back on the repair table again. Having located the fault and verified it, you should have stripped the unit, replaced the damaged element, and completely discarded the old one. In this way, you assure long and trouble-free service from the unit.

You must also learn to use and understand the materials and techniques that are available to you. For example, in attempting to solder aluminum with ordinary tin/lead solder and a soldering gun, you will have difficulty effecting a suitable bond because soldering to aluminum requires special materials and techniques. And soldering isn't always the "right way to go." Take the case of a broken heating element in a toaster. You may be able to stretch the wires over the break and solder them together. But when the toaster is plugged in and turned on, the heat of the element will certainly melt the solder, and there goes your break once again. Your effort will have accomplished nothing. The proper cure for this is to replace the element itself in its entirety. If you have an "emergency" situation, where guests are expected, you could use a metal crimp connector to effect a temporary repair.

In subsequent chapters, you will learn the essentials of using tools and of safety, so we won't dwell on those topics here. But you should learn safe working habits that will stand you in good stead and protect you. These are habits, and there's no room in the business of repairs for the smart aleck or "wise guy." Work carefully, thoughtfully, and safely and *never* work when you are tired.

Now let's take a look at an overview of small appliance repair before we dive right in.

The appliance once worked. Your job is to find out what went bad and replace the bad part so that the appliance will work again. It's our job, in this book, to help you learn to diagnose, check your facts, and show you how to make that repair quickly and easily. It's really not an awesome or difficult task, and it's a job that you will find challenging and interesting, and certainly rewarding. If you still have doubts, consider this: The appliance that is out of service because of failure will have to be replaced anyway. In attempting to make a repair you don't have a thing to lose but time.

2
Safety First

There's no profit in attempting to repair an electrical appliance and winding up with an electric shock that can put you in the hospital — or perhaps worse. There are certain basic safety rules that we want to explain so that you won't get hurt. However, most people begin reading such rules, decide that they're "simple common sense," and dismiss them. But thousands of people — all with good, common sense — DO get hurt each year. We don't want you to become a statistic.

Your author has worked with electricity all his life and probably knows as much about it as anyone. Like fire, electricity is a good servant, but a hard master, and this writer has a healthy respect for it. Maybe I'm overly cautious, but I will not "fool around" where electricity is concerned, and I suspect everything of trying to electrocute me, given half a chance. People laugh at me when I short out an ordinary clip lead before picking it up. But I'd rather play it safe.

The fact of the matter is that 115 volts of alternating current can give you a nasty jolt, and given the proper circumstances, can kill you. One of the problems, of course, is that our muscles are controlled by impulses from the brain that are very like electricity. Take hold of the wrong wire, and your muscles quickly contract, gripping the wire even more tightly. Remember too, that your heart is a muscle. Let some unwanted electricity get to it and blood will stop circulating in your body. Electricity can cause such a seizure.

Don't get me wrong. I'm not saying that you should be frightened to death of electricity. I'm simply advising you to show proper respect for it, be suspicious of it, and be aware of it at all times. Don't give it the chance to make you sorry.

There are many ways in which you can help protect yourself from your own carelessness. Never work on a piece of equipment that is plugged in, unless you are making specific tests that require the unit to be under voltage. Remember too, that even though the switch is turned off, voltage can be present at the terminals if the line cord is connected.

The surface on which you are working should be of a nonconducting material. We've seen people actually trying to work on the stainless steel drainboard of their kitchen sinks, and this is just asking for trouble.

When you're working with the power on, always work with one hand, keeping your other hand either in a pocket or behind your back looped through your belt. If you should happen to come in contact with some voltage, and have one hand resting on a suitable ground, the voltage will go from the hand that's in contact with the live circuit, across your chest, to the ground. If you have only one hand in contact with the voltage, and the other NOT grounded, the voltage will go up your arm, but not through the chest cavity. You've got a better chance of living.

Never work alone. Make sure that there is somebody in the house with you and instruct them on how to pull the switch in case something happens to you. If you are in contact with electricity, you may not even be able to speak, as all of your muscles — including your vocal cord muscles — can become paralyzed.

Never work when you're tired. If an appliance breaks down, the time to fix it is not during the evening of a workday, but during the weekend when you are rested and refreshed. Fatigue can make victims of all of us.

In selecting your tools, anticipate trouble. Pliers and wire cutters should be equipped with insulated handles. If they did not come with insulated handles, you can purchase a set of slip-on handle insulators at very low cost. Similarly, screwdrivers must have insulated handles.

So far, we've been talking about YOUR safety, which of course must come first. However, there are other safety factors that should also be considered. Always take care in "undressing" a unit that you do not break or chip or scratch plastic cases, and that metal jackets aren't marred either. In working on a unit, never do anything until you have planned your actions and weighed all the consequences. A botched repair job can leave an appliance in worse condition than when you started your work. If you have to probe while voltage is turned on or move wires to see that they are making proper contact, always do so with an insulated tool. If you do this with a metal-bladed screwdriver, you can cause a short-circuit.

Your work area must also be protected. Your wife will not be pleased if your work has left the dining room table a mess of scratches!

You can avoid such problems by first spreading a few sheets of old newspaper on the table. With this protection, you can move things about, and if a rough metal edge catches anything, it will be that expendable newspaper.

Safety is not so much a set of rules as it is a way of working. After you have conscientiously practiced safe working methods, you will find that you automatically work safely. It becomes the only way you CAN work.

In working on small appliances, there are certain things you must be aware of, and watch out for. Electricity is certainly the number-one problem area, for you will, under certain conditions, be required to make tests with the voltage on and the protective covering removed from the unit. You must know where exposed "hot" wires and connections are and avoid these.

Another danger is sharp edges on tools and on equipment. You can jab a hole in your hand if a screwdriver slips. And a metal edge on a dress cover can be turned under to keep sharp edges from being exposed while a unit is in use, but the sharp edges may be exposed when the cover is removed. Some units also employ heat. Rotisseries, toaster ovens, electric irons, and toasters can all get hot. While they usually cool down quickly, some can remain quite hot.

You will also be using a tool called a soldering iron and while we'll show you how to use it correctly and safely in a later chapter, do keep in mind that it uses heat to do its work, and it should be lifted only by the insulated wood or plastic handle — never by its metal parts. When you put down the iron, place it in or on a suitable rest, or it will burn and char the surface on which it rests.

While we're discussing soldering irons and safety, never under any circumstances use what is called acid-core solder. This solder uses corrosive acids as a fluxing or cleaning material. It sputters and jumps and seems to take deadly aim for human eyes. It cannot only hurt you, but even if you make an adequate solder joint with acid-core solder, in time the acid residue will cause the joint to corrode and you have to solder the joint again. Acid-core solder is fine for plumbers and pipefitters. In our work, repairing small appliances, we're going to use rosin-core solder exclusively.

In the event that you do get a burn, treat it at once. If the burn is severe, by all means see a physician as quickly as possible. If it's a mild burn, you can apply any of several commercially available burn unguents. One of the best is a type containing tannic acid, but recently we've come upon one containing the juices of the aloe plant, and this is the best we've found. If the burn is very painful, immersing the burn area in cold water will assuage the pain. Also, as soon as the burned area is covered, the pain will be eased, but if the skin is broken, take care about what you use as a covering.

Cuts must also be treated quickly, and if bleeding occurs, first try to stop the bleeding, then determine whether or not to see a physician. If you decide not to, by all means apply a suitable antiseptic and covering. Always have a first-aid kit handy.

3
Tools You'll Need

To begin with, we must point out that there are tools and there are tools. Some of them are essential; others are nice-to-have conveniences. If you have the essential tools, you can get along without the convenience tools.

The essential tools will be discussed first. Under the general heading of screwdrivers, you'll want a fairly hefty one with a one-quarter-inch blade about six or eight inches long. For working in close quarters, you'll also want a one-quarter-inch driver with a short, stubby handle. You will also want a smaller, one-eighth-inch blade screwdriver, which will also serve for removing and replacing control knobs.

Many manufacturers also use Phillips-head screws, and you'll want a large Phillips driver for the big jobs as well as a smaller, one-eighth-tip Phillips driver for small screws. Finally, obtain a standard one-sixteenth-inch Allen wrench, which is a piece of hexagonal steel bent into an "L" shape, for removing small set screws.

Get a good pair of "gas" pliers. These can be either the locking variety, the slip-joint type, or best of all, the channel type that adjust to a multiplicity of sizes. You'll also have use for a pair of long-nose pliers for handling small parts. Some of these tools are equipped to do double duty. The slip-joint pliers are equipped with cutters at the sides for cutting heavy cable, and some long-nose pliers have side cutters for clipping wires. We do not approve of either, because the side cutters cost more, and are usually placed so far back on the pliers as to be ineffectual for most jobs. Instead, obtain a pair of diagonal cutters (called "Dykes" or "diags") and keep them handy on the workbench.

While you can remove insulation from a wire with an ordinary knife, a wire stripper becomes almost essential as a time- and labor-saving tool. You can get these in assorted types, the best usually being the spring-loaded plier types.

A mallet with interchangeable heads is another handy tool you'll want. And to help you in exploring heavily-wired circuits, a piece of plastic rod, ground to a rounded point at one end, will serve to keep your fingers away from where they do not belong.

Before we go further, let's talk about how to care for these tools, now that you've got them.

As soon as you unwrap your tools, apply a light coat of oil to them. This will

A typical hand-held V.O.M. Note that the selector switch on the front and the assortment of plug-ins for test prods provide a multiplicity of uses for this instrument.

prevent rust and keep the tools in good condition. We might also advise you to buy the best tools you can afford. The better grades of steel in tools will hold their shape, won't be subjected to damage as easily, and will last a good deal longer.

Keep your tools in a safe place, where they will be dry and not bang into each other.

Your next most important tool is the soldering iron. We prefer the two-speed guns that offer two levels of heat, depending upon how far back you pull the trigger switch. We like this tool because you don't have to wait for it to heat up. If you do not want to be limited by your nearness to a wall outlet, get yourself a short extension cord too.

Make sure that the tip is properly locked in the gun by tightening the knurled nuts that hold it down. Before heating the gun, dress the tip with a file so that all carbon build-up and oxidation are removed, and that the tip is smooth and shiny. Then plug in the gun and squeeze the trigger to apply heat. Touch the tip with your solder, and wipe with a soft cloth while the tip is still hot. The solder will coat the tip, preventing further oxidation, and help, to transfer heat more easily to the work surface. Coating the tip with solder is called "tinning" and it should be done before soldering.

To use the soldering gun hold the gun beneath the joint to be soldered and in contact with it. Apply a bit of solder so that the junction of tip to joint is "wet" and then allow the joint to heat. Apply additional solder to the joint above the tip. The hot joint will melt the solder and gravity will carry the molten solder down and through the connection. When the solder has completely flowed, remove the soldering gun and allow the joint to cool completely before moving it. If you allow the joint to move or if you haven't applied sufficient heat, the joint will be coarse and grainy instead of smooth. This is called a "cold solder joint." You can correct this by reheating the joint and allowing the solder to flow once again.

Another important tool is the "VOM" or volt-ohm-milliameter. It's not expensive; you can get one for less than ten dollars. Unfortunately, most people who use a VOM use it exclusively in its ohms mode, as continuity testers. We're going to show you here how to get all the value out of this tool that you pay for.

Place the meter switch on the ohms scale. You may have more than one scale for ohms, such as "Ohms × One" and "Ohms × Ten." On the first scale, "Ohms × One," the meter reading will be exactly the resistance shown. On "Ohms × Ten," you multiply the meter indication by ten to get the actual resistance.

Start by setting the zero. With the test leads not touching, use a small screwdriver to set the indicator needle at zero. You do this with the screw that is on the meter panel directly below the meter. Now touch the two leads together. The needle will swing up-scale as you do this, toward the "zero" indication on the meter face. Use the "Zero Adjust" knob on the meter to set the needle exactly on zero on the ohms scale of the meter. Now you can accurately measure resistance by touching one probe to one terminal and the other probe to the other terminal. The meter will tell you the resistance (if any) between the two terminals. Resistance is measured in ohms. The symbol for ohms is the Greek letter omega (Ω). If the two probes are touching and there is complete continuity of the circuit between them, the needle will swing up-scale, to the right. If the probes are separated and the circuit is open, the needle will remain at the left, at "infinity" (∞).

Using this device in this mode, by extrapolating a bit you can tell quickly and easily if a circuit has been interrupted when it shouldn't be by placing the test leads at either end of the circuit. If it is continuous, the circuit will be complete and the needle will move full-scale to the right.

You can also use the VOM to measure either AC or DC voltage. Set the mode switch at the highest scale indicated and apply the test leads. You will be able to read the voltage on the appropriate scale. DC voltage is always referenced to ground or the chassis or frame, so you can apply the black (negative) lead to any part of the frame and the red (positive) lead to the circuit under test.

To read current (amps) you must interrupt the circuit so that the meter is placed in series with the circuit — in line with it. You will probably not be taking current readings very often, if at all.

Your meter is a precision instrument and should be treated with the respect it deserves. When not in use, it should be left on the highest AC voltage scale or on "Off" if it has an off position. It should not be tossed haphazardly into a tool box. The meter has a battery in it which is used in the ohms mode, and if you leave the switch on ohms and the leads should happen to touch, you can quickly drain the battery.

Essentially, these are the tools you will need. In time, however, you may find it necessary to use additional tools, and you can acquire these as the need arises. It's the same with materials. When you work on a unit of any sort, you're going to want to leave it in like-new condition, not just in operating condition. One problem area is cracks in plastic housings. A good plastic cement will work wonders in restoring like-new condition to such cabinetry. Chromed surfaces will usually respond to a metal polish, and you can get a small electroplating kit for under ten dollars that will do nicely in restoring metal surfaces.

You're going to find excellent application for a standard set of nut drivers, and there's no question that you'll soon be looking at screw-holding screwdrivers that use a small clamping device to hold the screw at the end of the driver while you guide it into place.

While we're on the subject of accessories, by all means pick up a box of assorted hardware: screws, sheet-metal screws and nuts of various sizes, and lockwashers, because these things have a decided affinity for your workshop floor.

One necessity is good lighting. We prefer fluorescent lighting as it is less likely than incandescent lighting to cast shadows. You will want your work area in a location that is also well ventilated.

In testing an appliance, you're going to want to know if the full 115 volts AC is present where it is supposed to be. One of the handiest gadgets we've seen for this is a pen-sized handi-tester consisting of a clear plastic barrel, a metal prod, and a pocket clip. You hold one finger on the metal pocket clip, touch the prod to the suspect circuit, and if voltage is present, the neon lamp inside the plastic barrel will light up.

Another handy device is a pop rivet tool. Some appliances are held together with rivets, and while you can remove a rivet by drilling or filing it off, replacing it can be a problem. We use the pop rivet tool, which forms the rivet securely, all from one side, without the danger or noise of the explosive cherry rivets.

As you get more deeply involved in repair work, the need for other tools will arise. You can always fill in the gaps in your tool kit when the need arises and you should not feel under pressure to buy more tools than you need before you require them.

4
Fault Analysis

Try to find out precisely what took place that led to the conclusion that the appliance isn't working. Did it stop with a bang? Did it spit and spark? From where? Did it smoke? All of these things can be indicators of the sort of trouble you are going to run up against. Whatever it did, stay cool. Be calm. Be methodical.

If an electrical appliance shows no signs of life whatever, first make sure that it is plugged into a live outlet. If the outlet is not putting out any voltage, you can assume that a fuse blew out. Should this be the case, remove some of the other appliances from the same circuit to lighten the overload before replacing the fuse, or your new fuse will also blow. Fuses don't "get weak" or "wear out." A fuse is good until it gets hit with an overload, and then it must be replaced.

Frequently, an appliance will exhibit signs that it is getting proper voltage even though it isn't working. An electric fan, for example, might hum and strain, but not rotate. What might be the problem here is that the motor needs lubricating. Your course of action in a case like this is to unplug the unit. If you leave a bound motor plugged in, it can burn out. Now try to force the blade to rotate with your hand. Look for two or more small holes marked "oil" and do just that with some light machine oil or household oil. If such holes are not visible, apply a couple of drops to where the motor shaft emerges from the bushing and allow gravity to take its course by tipping up the fan. Continue trying to rotate the blade to free the stuck motor shaft, then remove the housing and get at the other end of the shaft. Frequently, the old oil will turn to sludge and some fresh oil can loosen things up just enough to restore operation. Once you've got the blades moving freely, always dry off the excess oil before turning on the fan, or you'll get oil-splattered.

The electric company can sometimes be blamed for appliance failures. If you look at the identification tag on any appliance, you'll usually see "90-120 volts AC." That means that the appliance is designed to work on any voltage between 90 and 120. Rare indeed will be the time that the voltage goes that high, let alone higher, but it certainly can go below the 90-volt mark. During summer energy crises, your local electric company may deliberately reduce the line voltage, but probably not below 90 volts. A high-resistance short in your circuit can pull the voltage down too, and your electric company will be delighted to know about this before real trouble occurs. So don't hesitate to pull out your VOM, set it for the highest range of AC volts, and stick the prods into your wall outlet. If the voltage is low, call the electric company. They can install a chart recorder that will tell them when and if voltage lows are reached in your home. When the line voltage is excessively low, heating units may not heat sufficiently, motors may not operate properly or at all, and lights may not glow quite as brightly as they are supposed to.

Your own attitude in approaching a repair job is very important. Many people begin by ripping into a unit in the hope that they will see something obviously wrong. However, it's a far better approach to consider in advance what might possibly be wrong and then methodically, by the process of elimination, to verify or contradict your suspicions.

When you purchase an appliance, you usually receive along with it an exploded view diagram which lists all the component parts and part numbers. This diagram is a valuable aid in reassembling the unit. Should you lose your information sheet, write to the manufacturer for another copy, giving him the name and model number of the appliance. The manufacturer will probably be able to provide another copy for you. When a single component or an entire subassembly must be replaced, use the manufacturer's part number when ordering a part. If a service center near your home is authorized to make repairs on your particular appliance, do not hesitate to visit it. Cultivate the friendship of its personnel and they will be more than willing to sell you the parts and give valuable advice in making repairs.

Before we begin, stop to consider that when you buy a replacement part or component, it had better be an exact duplicate of the part you are taking out. Frequently, completely dissimilar parts can LOOK alike but not function correctly when installed. We've seen cases where an experienced technician could substitute parts with parts made by different manufacturers by modifications to the appliance so that it would accommodate the different parts. We do not recommend this course of action, as it is totally unsuited to the home do-it-yourselfer. Make certain when you buy a replacement component or subassembly that the part number on the box is identical to the part you have removed. This is the only certain way to know that you are buying an replacement.

You may sometimes buy a replacement part not from the manufacturer, but from an original parts supplier. If so, he will publish a list of all the components that he makes, with a corresponding list of the components they can replace. A typical listing from such a parts manufacturer might look like this:

"P-0159...Replaces GE-3776, 2078, Westinghouse R-111." This component can be used as a completely interchangeable component with those that the parts manufacturer says he can replace.

Another problem area for most beginners is stripping the appliance to get at the innards. Do this with as much deliberation as you can. The dress covering is meant to be removed and should not have to be forced. Smaller appliances with plastic covers often have little lugs that can be pryed away to permit the cover to be lifted off. Sometimes you have to remove knobs from control shafts so that the cover can be taken away. On some units, especially those with metal covers, sheet metal screws will be used to hold the cover in place. Proceed cautiously and know what you are going to do before you do it.

5
Electric Motors in General

The electric motor is a transducer that takes electrical energy and converts it to rotating mechanical energy. A transducer is any device that takes one form of energy and converts it to another form of energy. The electric motor takes electrical energy and converts it to mechanical energy. Conversely, the electric generator takes mechanical energy and converts it to electrical energy. A loudspeaker in a radio is a transducer, for it converts electrical energy to audio energy. The microphone converts audio energy to electrical... and the common light bulb converts electrical energy to light energy. The electric power to the motor is brought to the brushes which are usually small carbon contacts that ride on the segmented commutator. This brings the electricity to the armature, which is a coil of wire attached to the motor shaft, which rotates inside the field windings that surround it. The field windings are also called the "stator" windings because they do not move. When an electric current passes through a wire coil, the coil becomes magnetized. Because alternating current is constantly changing direction, the field windings and the armature windings push and pull, and the magnetic field causes the armature to rotate.

Most motors are equipped with bushings that support the armature shaft. On the smaller motors, these bushings are formed of "oilite," a lubricant-impregnated porous bronze material. It's always a good idea to apply a bit of oil to both the front and back bearings. But don't overdo it, because we do not want the motor soaked with oil. Some of the larger motors are equipped with small holes for applying oil, and those holes will be marked with the word "oil."

The commutator is a segmented hub that fits over one end of the motor shaft and consists of brass or copper strips separated by insulating material. To inspect the commutator, you must first remove the brushes, which are fitted, horizontally opposed, under screw-on caps at the end of the motor shaft. Unscrew the caps carefully and remove the brushes. These are held with springs and must be removed with care. If heavy wear is obvious, the brushes should be replaced. While you have the brushes out, clean and inspect the commutator too.

Make certain that the commutator surface is clean and free of chips that might short two of the segments. Any such chips should be carefully picked away. We have cleaned badly-used commutators by placing the entire armature in a drill press, turning it on, and holding a strip of fine emery cloth against the spinning unit. After such treatment, always clean the commutator thoroughly.

Now reassemble the armature to the field windings, making certain that the rear end of the armature shaft enters the rear bushing. Put the brushes into place, and the motor can now be tested.

Some of the major problems with motors arise from dirt and grit that interfere with the rotation of the armature. When dirt builds up or there is a lack of proper lubrication, the shaft will bind and the motor will not rotate, causing the magnetic fields to buck and the coils to burn out. Before a motor burns out, it gets good and hot. Some motors are protected by small thermostatic fuses that, when the motor overheats, will open the circuit and cut off the electricity. When the motor cools down, the thermostat closes and the motor operates once more. This "on-and-off" operation indicates that overheating is occurring and that servicing (usually lubrication and cleaning) is required.

The other big problem motors have occurs when the brushes wear down to the point where only the springs that hold them in place are in contact with the commutator. Whenever you have occasion to take down the motor, always inspect the brushes and be sure that sufficient material remains to operate the motor properly. If it does not, you will have to replace the brushes.

The brushes are usually held in place by small plastic caps that fit at each side of the motor on the commutator end. Unscrew these caps carefully so that the springs and the old brushes do not fly away. Remove the old brushes and insert new ones. Replace the springs and caps. You may find that the new brushes, especially on smaller motors, come as complete units with the springs attached. In this case, you can discard the old springs.

If you remove the armature to clean the commutators, by all means remove the brushes first, for you will be unable to replace the armature without first removing the brushes.

The U.L. Knot.

This is a special sort of knot that is used in wire to serve as a strain relief. Characteristic of this knot is that the more strain you place on it, the tighter it becomes. Use this knot whenever you have a wire coming from an appliance or into a plug. It's easy to learn to tie, simply by following the illustrations herewith:

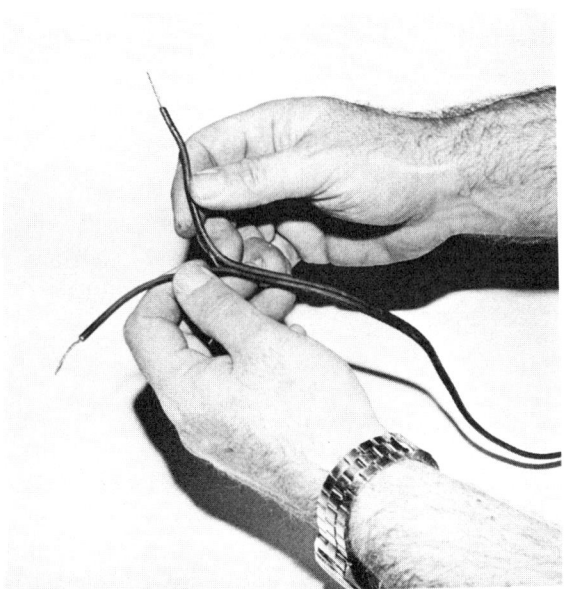

To tie a U.L. Knot, begin by separating the "zip cord" wires for a length of two inches.

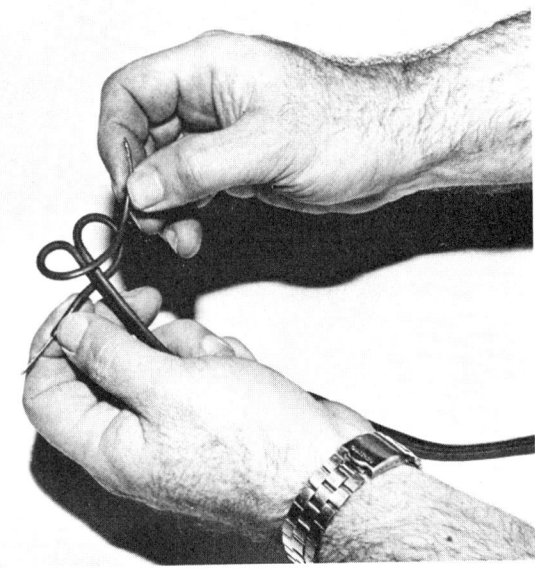

Loop one end around the front and one end around the back.

Electric Motors in General

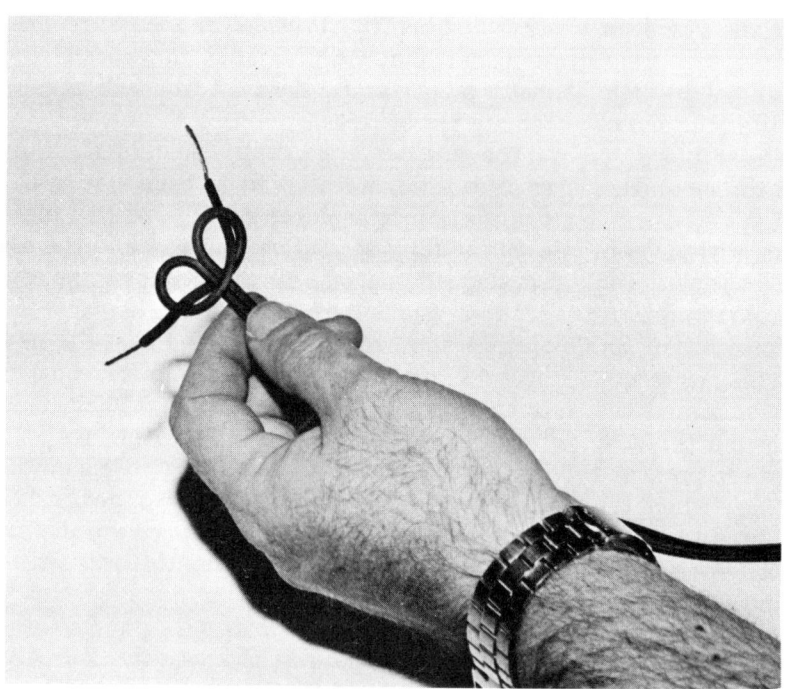

Place the two ends of the wires through the loops toward which they are pointed.

Pull the ends tight.

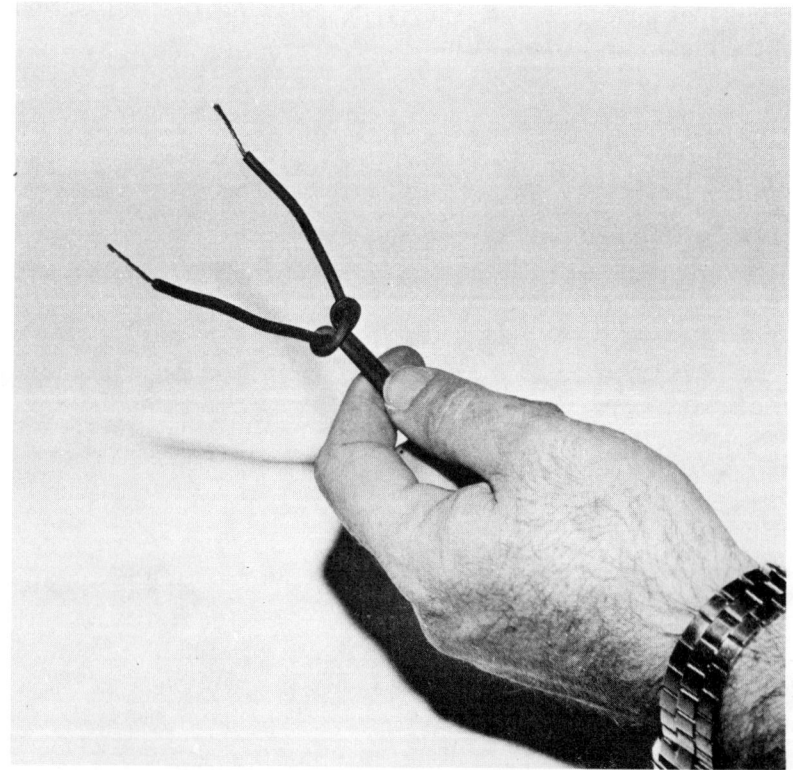

18 Small Appliance Repair

6
Electric Toasters

As you can imagine, the various component parts of a toaster are mass-produced in order to make the units at an economically-feasible price. When you build a toaster in this way, some of the parts can wear at unpredictable rates. What's more, because electro-mechanical parts are often subject to the condition of the atmospheres in which they operate, the very air around them can cause problems. Urban areas with high sulphur dioxides will cause moving electromechanical parts to go faster than the same unit that is used in a suburban or rural area. Preventive maintenance of course, is the key. Regularly inspect these components and where a build-up of oxidation is seen on electro-mechanical contacts, remove such oxides regularly, burnishing the contacts with a mildly abrasive pumice, finish the burnishing with brown wrapping paper, and the unit will continue to function well. You see, as the oxides build up on contact surfaces, the contact no longer functions over the entire surface, causing all the electricity to flow on a small portion of the contact surface. This results in arcing or sparking and subsequent uneven wear.

The operating mechanism that lifts the toast when it is finished, is worked by a system of springs that are carefully balanced to do their job. Because these springs are subjected to a great deal of heat, they can sometimes be annealed and will take a "set" that prevents them from working. The springs can also stretch out of shape, to the point where they no longer function properly. To correct this condition, first establish that it exists by seeing to it that the toaster is free of obstructions, such as crumbs. Now apply light finger pressure to "assist" the spring in doing its job. If the unit works with this added impetus from your finger, the spring should be replaced. However, before replacing the spring, try this step:

Unhook the spring from its anchor, around which the last loop of the spring will be hooked. Now shorten the spring by cutting off about one-quarter of it using an ordinary wire cutters. Using a long-nose pliers, bend the remaining loops to the right angle away from the body of the spring, and hook the shortened spring over the anchor. You may find that the shortened spring has increased tension, and is better able to do the job. This might save you a trip hunting for the correct spring, as well as the cost of a replacement. Such a

At either side of the heater basket, you'll find wires from the control switch that are screw-connected to the basket. Remove these wires, taking care not to lose the small nut and lockwasher underneath.

With the wires disconnected, the entire basket can be lifted out for repair, cleaning, or part replacement.

stop-gap repair can work for a good, long time.

The plug at the end of the electric cord on your toaster can go bad, as can the entire cord assembly. If the unit fails to operate at all, use a tester to determine that the electricity has indeed a clean path to the operating mechanism. If it does not, you will want to replace the entire cord. This must be an exact replacement, too. If the old cord was an asbestos-insulated one, by all means replace it with an asbestos-insulated cord! You may find that the old cord was connected by rivets. Remove the old rivets either by drilling them out or by filing down the heads until the shank of the rivet pops out to release the wires. Connect the replacement wires using small bolts, nuts, flatwashers and lock washers, or by using a riveting tool to replace the rivets you removed. Always twist the strands of the replacement wire so none of them reach out and touch the metal covering or the other terminal. To keep the twisted strands from unravelling, pass them around the connector (screw or rivet) in a clockwise direction.

7
Toaster Ovens

Electrically, as the unit ages, you may find that there's a lot of arcing as the oven cycles on and off. This is usually caused by a collection of dirt and oxides on the terminals of the operating switches. You can usually correct such arcing by simply cleaning the contacts with a bit of emery cloth, and finish the polishing of the contacts with some ordinary brown paper. If the arcing continues, or if you cannot (or prefer not to) clean the contacts, the switch mechanism can be replaced, and replacement parts are available from your local manufacturer's repair department at nominal cost.

We have seen another problem with toaster ovens, in that the mechanical mechanism will bind and not properly release when the food inside is ready. This is usually a mechanical problem caused by binding that results from wear on the mechanical latches and related parts. To correct this condition, examine the operating parts. You may find that a metal burr has formed. If so, use a fine file and dress the metal down on both sides to remove the burr, then use a rat-tail file to dress the operating mechanism back to proper shape. Try the unit several times to make sure that it is working, and if not, use the files once again. However, keep in mind that you can remove metal with the file, but you can't put it back! When you are satisfied that the release is operating properly, finish the job by applying a bit of high-temperature grease to the unit and check it a few more times to work the grease into position.

While these units are fairly well protected against dead short circuits, any electrical appliance can develop these problems. These problems are evident when the house fuses or circuit breakers pop as the unit is plugged in, or when it is turned on. First ascertain that you have not overloaded the line by operating too many appliances at once. When you are assured of this, plug the toaster oven in once again and see if the fuse goes. If it does, the problem, obviously, is in the A.C. line and connection before the "start" switch has been reached. If the fuse pops *after* the start switch is pressed, the problem will be between the switch and the balance of the circuit.

In the former case, where the problem seems to be in the line itself, check the wall plug to see that it is properly wired. People are prone to yank electrical cords from outlets by pulling on the cord and weaken the connection to the plug. If this is where the problem seems to be, cut the plug away, re-strip the

Whenever you have occasion to service a toaster oven, make it a point to apply some oil to all parts where metal bears on metal.

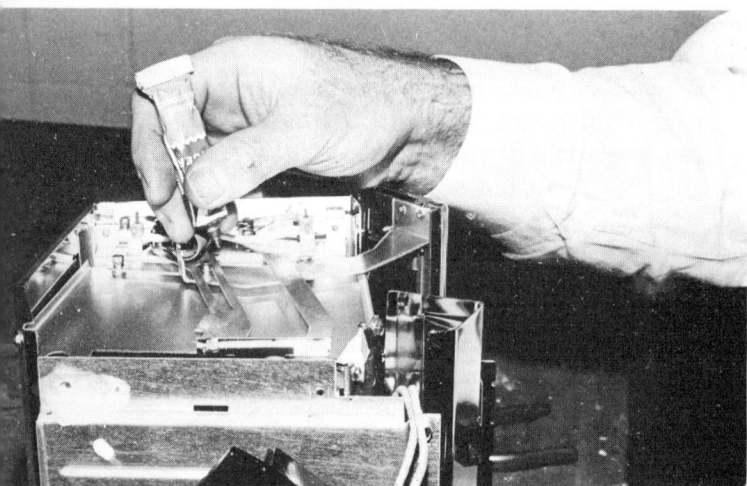

Where heavier friction may occur, use a heavier grade of lubricant. Light machine grease is used here.

A small stud acts as a stop for the opening of the lid. The stud is insulated by a rubber bumper sleeve. Rotate this sleeve if the sleeve appears worn.

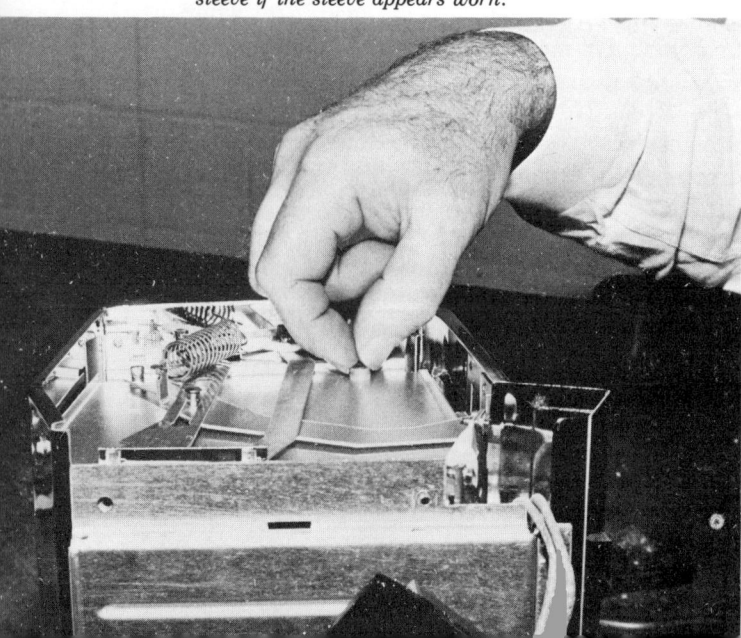

wires and put the plug back properly. At the same time, check the wiring of the line cord into the oven. You may locate your short right there. A "short circuit" is precisely what the name implies. The two wires conducting the electricity into the unit have touched so that the applied electricity has a direct path without servicing the unit, and this will cause the fuse to blow. If you see this condition, simply separate the wires and you will have corrected the fault.

If the fault occurs beyond the switch and into the unit, you'll have to locate the problem visually, but a small continuity tester will help to isolate the fault.

Be careful however. In most homes, one side of the A.C. line is at ground potential, the other side is "hot." If your unit has a short because the "hot" side of the line has grounded to the cabinet, you might be safe as long as the plug is connected to the wall outlet "ground-to-ground." If you reverse the plug, you could get an electric shock! Such shorts can be checked for by placing one lead of your continuity tester (ohmeter) on one end of the plug, the other end on the metal covering of your oven. If you get no reading, try with the lead on the other end of the plug. Still no reading? You're okay. If you *do* get a reading, don't plug the unit in again until you clear the short.

Some of these units have a "three-pin" plug with a grounded pin for protection. Do *not* remove this ground pin! To do so could subject you to electric shock. If your outlets are the duplex type that do not have a grounded connector, simply get an adapter which is easy to install, or change the outlet to one that will accept the three-pin plug.

8
Electric Clocks

The motor in an electric clock is of a synchronous type, which means that it senses the 60 cycles in the alternating current. Because this 60 cycles is highly accurate, the electric clock operates with amazing accuracy. Unfortunately, when an electric clock fails, it's usually because the motor has burned out and there is little you can do to effect a repair other than replace the motor or the clock.

Usually, before an electric clock dies completely, it will give some warning in the form of noise. It will buzz, hum, or otherwise indicate to you that it is in trouble. What it's trying to tell you is that it requires lubrication and/or cleaning.

When you start hearing strange noises from your clock, turn it upside down. Let it run for a week in that position, and then turn it right side up. Chances are that the noise will have disappeared.

You see, lubricants follow the law of gravity, and after operating for a long time in the same position, all the lube settles at the bottom. When you invert the clock, you give the lubricant a chance to run back through the works, where it can settle in place.

There is one more case that's worth talking about here. Let's assume you have a clock that is a treasured family possession and the electric motor finally malfunctions. You want to restore the clock to operation.

Start out with a new fit-up. This is a clock motor without a dial, hands or case. If your local dealer can't get one for you, buy a new electric clock and take it apart to get the fit-up.

Remove the old fit-up from the clock, mount the new one in its place, and replace the hands. Now your family heirloom will function like new for a long time.

If you haven't been able to get the clock to work properly with these ministrations, you have nothing to lose with the following steps:

Determine whether the problem is in the motor or in the gearing mechanism that operates the clock. You can usually do this by freeing the motor from the gears. This will require that you break the gear train by removing one of the gears that is driven by the motor itself. Do not attempt to remove the drive gear connected to the motor shaft, as this is usually a tight shrink fit. Instead,

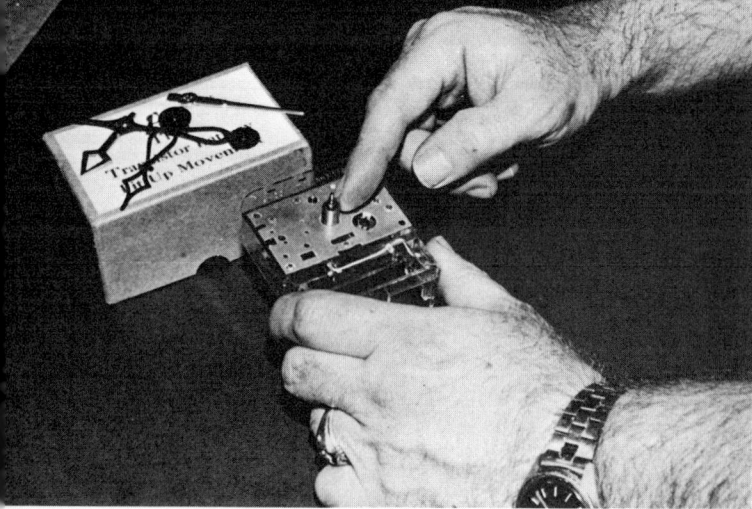
The fit-up has a threaded shaft (shown here) that mounts the motor to the face of the new clock.

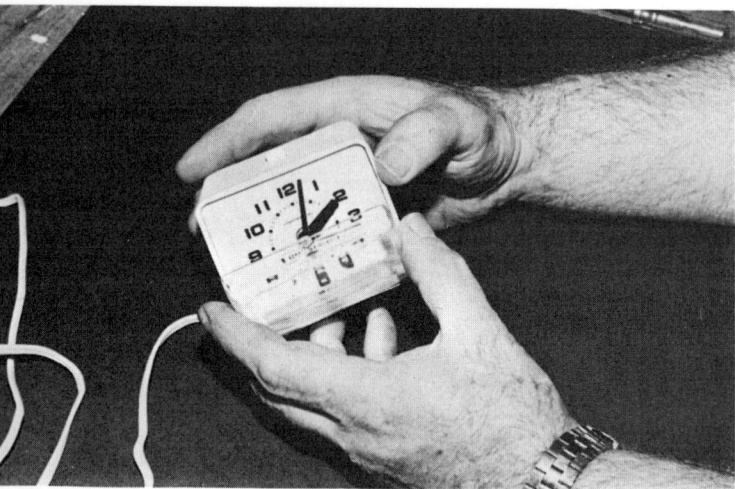
The glass (or plastic) cover of an electric clock is simply popped out of the case to provide access to the hands.

The hands are removed by rotating in the direction of the split ring at the center, and can then easily be lifted away.

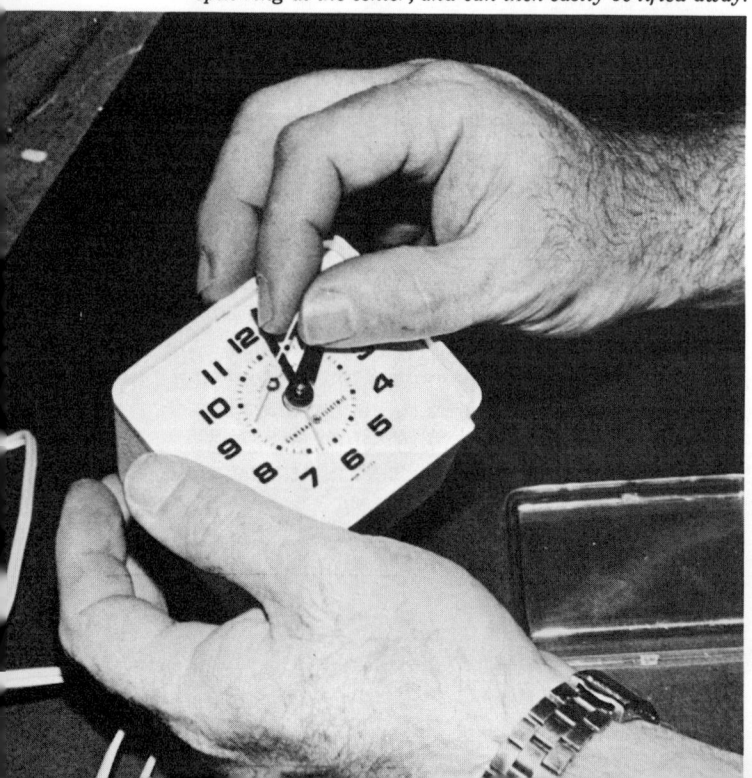

locate the gear that this one drives and remove it. How? Usually, this is a thin steel blank whose teeth ride in the drive gear on the motor shaft. It couples through pawls and escapements to the balance wheel. Use a jeweler's loupe or a magnifier to remove the clip that holds this gear in position. The gear should lift right out.

With this gear removed, plug in the clock and observe the motor shaft. If it operates, it indicates that the fault is in the gear train, not in the motor. If it does not operate, the motor must be replaced by a like motor in good operating condition.

If the trouble is not in the motor (evidenced by the fact that the motor is operating properly), you have to work from the hands backward to locate the source of binding in the gear train. Sometimes this is obvious and evident. A clock can be dropped and this can cause a gear to go out of alignment. When cocked, it will bind up the works in short order. You must locate such a fault and correct it.

Someone playing with a clock can bend the hands in such a way that one hand engages the other so that the clock cannot function. Straightening the hands will often correct such a fault.

On some clock mechanisms, you have to remove the hands to get the works out of the clock case. There are two common methods for mounting the hands of a clock.

You may find a small knurled nut over the center shaft. By loosening and removing this nut, you can lift the hands off the clock. Other clocks do not have such a nut, but the mount of the hands has a small cut running from the center hole to the perimeter and the hands are pressed over the shaft. Lift off the hands, grasping them one at a time by the center mount.

There is a firm that can supply complete clock mechanisms of all types and sizes. It offers pendulum movements, electric battery types, wind-ups, and a wide assortment of clock faces and hands, should you have to replace those:

Lanshire Clock & Instrument Co.
c/o Empire
1295 Rice St.
St. Paul, MN 55117

Write for their catalogs. Using these new fit-ups, as they are called, you can replace the existing clockwork mechanism with one that works. This company is the clock repairman's best friend. Prices are reasonable, and with the equipment they offer, it's often easier to refit than to repair.

Regulating a watch or clock can best be done by a watchmaker who is equipped with devices that pulse the watch or clock and count the beats per second. Many newer watches and clocks are self-regulating. If the watch or clock runs too fast, turn the hands back to the correct time and the watch or clock will also retard. When the amount of retardation or advancement is too small to be meaningful, allow the time to accumulate for a few days before you reset the timepiece.

One of the most common failings of a wristwatch or pocket watch is that it becomes overwound. Do not attempt to open such a watch if it is a water-resistant type because you will destroy the seal. To get such a watch working, first try — carefully — to wind the watch. Do *not* attempt to force the crown if the watch is overwound. If you cannot get the crown to move even a single notch, this indicates overwinding. Hold the watch flat and level; then with a quick flick of your wrist, rotate the watch with a "snap." This should start the balance wheel to moving and bleed some of the energy out of the main spring. The watch should operate for a moment and then stop. Repeat this many times, each time taking some of the energy out of the spring until the balance wheel operates without stopping.

9
Electric Carving Knives

The electric carving knife is such a simple mechanism that, with ordinary preventive maintenance, nothing should go wrong with it. The usual maintenance needed is proper cleaning and keeping the blades sharp.

Here's an important bit of information that many people overlook. Getting replacement parts is often next to impossible, so when you buy a new appliance, always try to get the same make and model. Keep the old one. If (for example) the blade release gives up and dies on your first electric knife, you might be able to salvage all the other still-working parts when you have problems with the new one! It's an economical solution to a ticklish problem.

If your knife has a serrated blade, detach the blade and sharpen it using a wheel-type sharpener of the abrasive type. You can usually find a suitable sharpener in any hardware store. Try to get the kind into which you insert the blade, then roll back and forth. Do not use a pull-through steel sharpener on serrated blades.

Should your unit fail to eject the blade, disconnect the wall plug and try to pull the blade free while pressing the ejector button. Once the blade has been removed, the unit should be completely cleaned and lubricated. Separate the plastic halves of the handle and make sure that the ejector unit is functioning properly. The pressure springs have been known to slip aside so that the ejector will not operate. You can correct this during reassembly.

If the motor fails to operate, check the switch to make sure that it is functioning; if it is, try rotating the motor shaft with your fingers. If this turns freely, you may have a burned-out winding in the motor. If this is the case, replace the motor if one is available.

To check the switch on an electric knife, open the unit after unplugging it, and place your ohmmeter test leads so that each test lead touches one terminal of the switch. Now operate the switch. When you press the switch, the indicator needle of your ohmmeter should rise to full conductance.

Generally, these units employ nylon gears, cams, and actuators. It is possible that, in time, these can wear down and break. Usually, when such a part fails, it shatters.

Unfortunately, the only source for replacements will be an authorized dealer or service shop. If you bring the unit in and show them what's wrong, they will generally sell you a replacement part rather than take the unit in for service. Remember that your warranty is then voided.

Before you install the new part, you'll have to be sure that all of the old part has really disappeared. Check the mounting hub and spindle assemblies to see that there are no residual pieces left in place. Then — and only then — should you proceed to install the new part.

Fitting the new part usually is not a difficult task. It will either be held in place with set screws, or may be force-fitted. If set screws are used, position the new part on the spindle and fasten the screws. If it's a force-fit, you'll have to remove the operating assembly and press the new part into position.

Some electric carving knives have rechargeable batteries in them, and the knife can be placed in a special holder which recharges the batteries. If the batteries are completely drained, establish that the holder is plugged into a suitable live outlet, and that the knife unit is resting properly in the holder to allow the batteries to recharge.

Once the batteries have drained off completely, it will take a while to recharge them. You'll want to leave the unit plugged in at least twenty-four hours for the cells to recharge. To avoid this, keep the holder plugged in all the time. The drain is less than would be required by an electric clock and it could save you woes in battery replacement later.

In some cases, once the batteries have been fully drained, they cannot be reformed, and have to be replaced. Open the handle, disconnect the old batteries, and replace them with new ones. The batteries usually have copper solder tabs to which you will have to make a soldered connection.

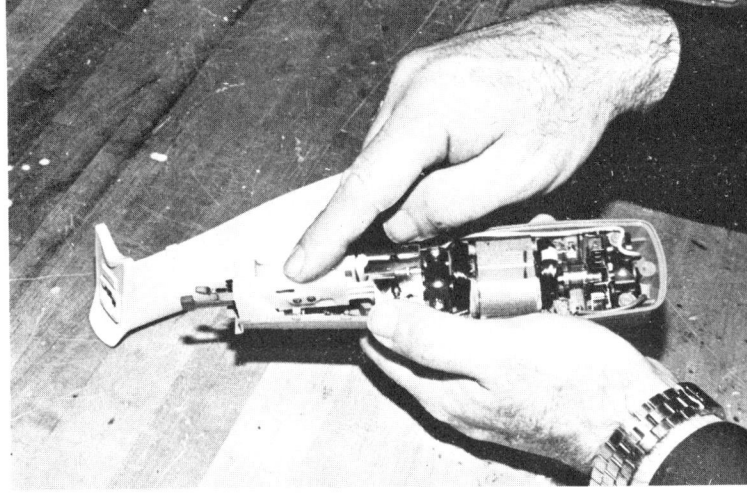

The two parallel runners will need some light grease. Work it into place by rotating the motor shaft.

Apply a drop of light oil to the motor bushing.

If the brushes are in need of changing, first unsolder the fine wire that connects to the brush holder. Lift the wire aside, change the brushes, and re-solder the wire.

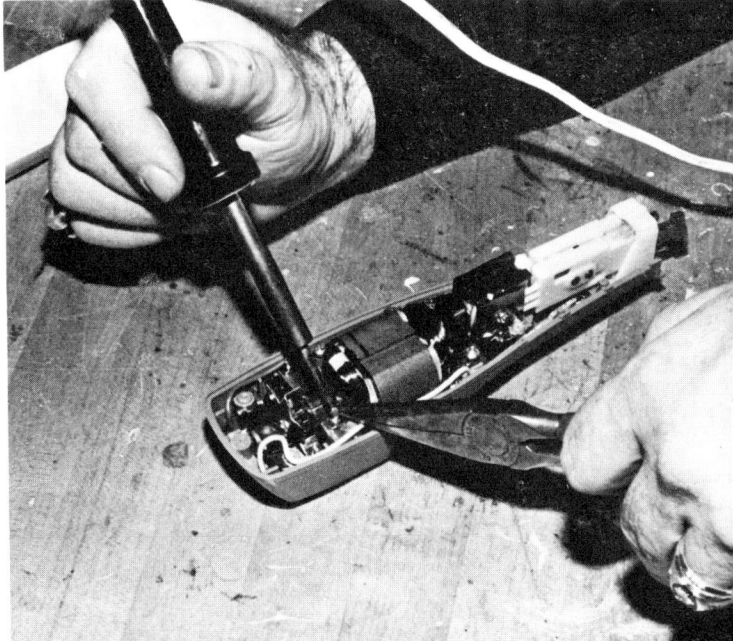

10
Meat Slicers

There would be a lot less trouble with electric meat slicers if people would just take the trouble to bone the meat before slicing it. The blade can become dull after trying to saw its way through a bony roast. Therefore, your biggest problem will be keeping the blade sharp. Fortunately, we've discovered a neat little trick that will do the job nicely. If you examine the blade you will see that it is circular and that it is attached by way of a keyed slot to the armature shaft of the driving motor. Furthermore, the blade is flat on one side and sharpened to a bevel at the other side.

Let's take the case of a meat slicer that has been dulled by hard use. There are no deep nicks in the blade, no gouges where it bit into a piece of bone, and no spots that have been carved out in its outer edge by snagging a fork held carelessly in the hand. To restore such a blade to sharpness, obtain a scissor sharpener formed from a carborundum stone. You'll observe that this type of stone has a flat plastic guide and a beveled honing edge. Carefully wet the carborundum, turn on the motor, and lift the guard to expose the blade edge. Hold the stone against the beveled edge of the blade lightly, and allow the rotating blade to sharpen itself against the stone. Keep wetting the stone with ordinary tap water.

When you have achieved the degree of sharpness you desire, hold the flat side of the blade against the flat side of the stone, and run the blade once more to remove all burrs.

Carefully remove the blade and wash and wipe it dry. This will remove any residual carborundum that may have become implanted in the steel.

If the blade looks as if it had been used by ancient gladiators to parry heavy blows with a battle axe, more drastic steps will have to be taken. Check the depth of the gouges and if they are less than one-sixteenth of an inch, you may be able to restore the blade rather than replace it.

You do essentially the same thing as before, but before you begin, hold a square carborundum stone against the edge of the rotating blade just as though you were deliberately trying to dull the blade. This will create a square edge on the blade but it will also remove the nicks. When all the nicks and gouges are gone, go through the resharpening steps outlined above to restore the blade to a useable edge once again.

Electrically, the meat slicer is not a complex machine. An on-off switch controls the motor operation and the motor turns the blade. Mechanically, too, the device is nothing more than a support on which the meat to be sliced is driven by simple hand pressure against a fixed guide and then moved back and forth under the blade.

If the motor operates and the blade is honed, the machine will operate. If the motor does not operate, unplug the unit from the wall and open the motor housing by removing the mounting screws that hold it in position on the slicer. Determine that power is able to get to the motor itself by placing one test prod of your ohmmeter on the motor terminal, the other on one of the prongs of the AC line cord, then operate the switch. If you do not get any response, try the other prong and repeat. Do the same thing again at the other motor terminal to ensure that the connections are continuous. If this does not help, it might indicate the need to replace the switch, which could be faulty. Remove the old switch by disconnecting it, and unscrew the hexagonal nut that holds it in position. Place the ohmmeter leads across the switch, and operate the switch. It *should* show continuity in one switch position, no continuity in the other switch position.

If replacement is required, obtain a similar switch at your local parts shop, replace it, and you will have the unit working once again.

If the moving parts do not function because they are bound, you will have to completely clean the unit. Saturate the unit with alcohol while applying pressure to the moving parts. When they have been freed sufficiently to allow movement, take the entire assembly apart by removing the holding nuts at the ends. Using a straight alcohol solution, remove all dirt and grease until the metal parts are bright once again. Stubborn spots might require some treatment with a fine emery paper, used wet.

When the unit is completely cleaned, wipe on a covering of light machine oil to restore like-new operation, then reassemble the unit.

11
Vibrators

There are essentially two basic types of vibrators that you will come into contact with: one type operates like an electric buzzer; the other type contains a small but powerful electric motor that drives an eccentric cam causing the vibrations.

To diagnose the trouble with your machine, begin by unplugging the unit from the wall outlet and removing the covering by taking the mounting screws out. Look for the obvious first: burned or disconnected wires, loose components, etc. If the unit is a buzzer type, make sure that all the exposed contacts are clean. Use a piece of brown wrapping paper to burnish the contact points. Rub the paper briskly over the contacts, and for an even better job, spray the contacts with contact cleaner solution, obtainable at your local electronics shop.

Now manually depress the operating contact against the coil. It should move easily and freely. If it does not, see if the hinged side is free and able to move. If it is not, apply a bit of lubrication at the hinge. If this contact is simply resting in the pulled-in position, make sure that the tension spring (near the hinge) is tight and in proper position.

If this fails to restore the unit to operation, chances are that the coil itself has opened. The only way to repair this is to replace the entire coil, obtainable from an authorized service center for that unit.

The motor-driven types are another story. Open the housing and see that the vibrating cam is in place and secure. Two small set screws are used to hold this in position and sometimes the vibrations can loosen the screws. If this takes place, the motor will turn but no vibration will occur. A small Allen wrench will put things to rights for you.

Another problem these units come up against is that the wire springs designed to go over the hands may either break loose of their moorings, or may stretch and require replacement. If they come loose, you must open the case and replace the hooks under the lips of the case edge, securing the springs as they were before.

When the springs stretch the best and surest cure is to replace them. However, if the stretched area is near the mounting hooks, you can often save some time and money by disconnecting the spring that has stretched and then use a strong wire cutter to clip away the stretched portion. Bend the next to the last spring loop at right angles and refasten it to the mounting hook. Do not be concerned that the repaired spring will be "tighter" than the others when in the relaxed position. When you stretch the springs over your hand, they will adjust to the correct size.

Some vibrators are designed to accept various adapters or massage heads. While most of these are formed of soft rubber, they have been known to wear and not remain in place in the vibrator's chuck. Generally, there will be one head you use frequently, which will be the one most apt to erode. Another head, one you employ less often, will have a shank and adapter almost like new.

It's a relatively simple matter to use a sharp blade and cut the shanks off both, discarding the worn shank, and then, using a polymeric cement, attach the new shank to the old head. Make sure that you cut the full length of the shank for best results.

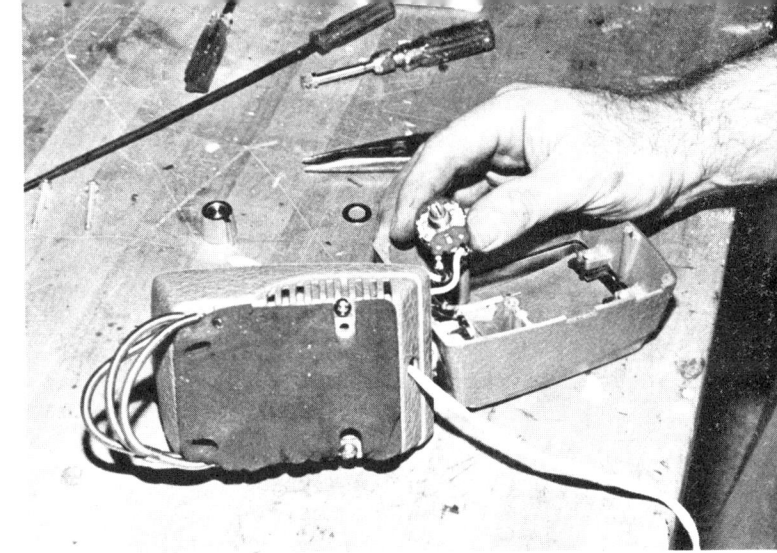

The potentiometer of a vibrator can go bad. To replace, pull the knob off, remove the mounting nut, and then unsolder the old pot. Replace it with an exact duplicate from your electronics supplier.

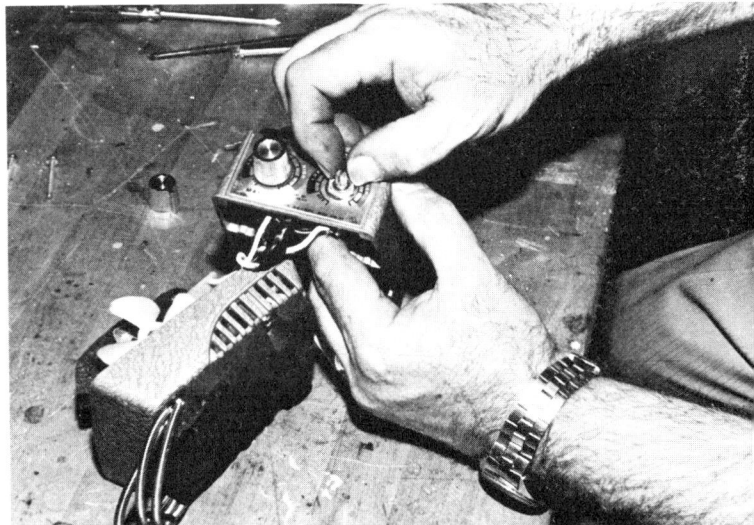

After soldering the wires in place, remount the new unit and tighten the holding nut. Press the knob back in place.

While you've got the unit apart, apply a few drops of light machine oil to the eccentric weights that provide the vibration.

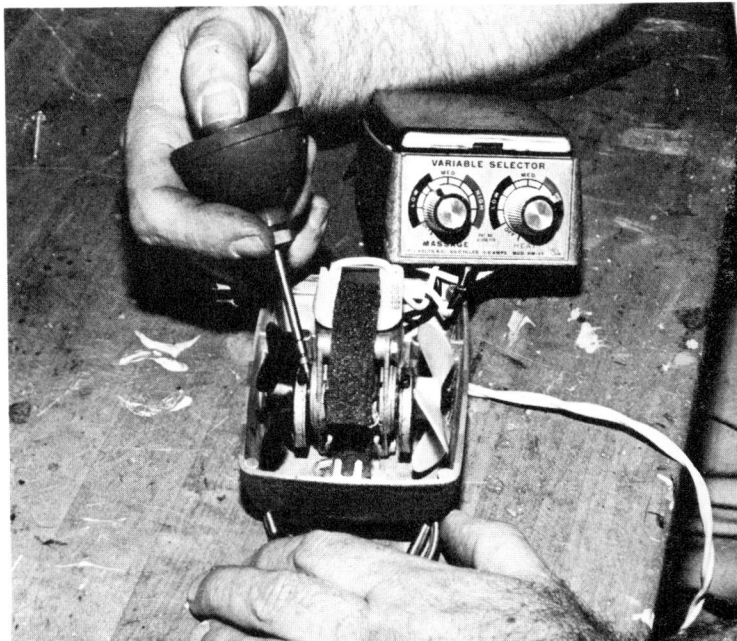

12
Vacuum Cleaners

To analyze the misfunction here, run down the following points. If the motor operates properly, but the machine doesn't pick up dirt, or if placing your hand over the intake doesn't indicate the presence of a suction of air, there are certain things you should do before taking the unit apart. First, change the bag. If the bag is filled with dirt or if dirt is clogged around the lower end of the bag, the vacuum cleaner won't suck up the dirt. The next step is to disassemble all the accessory hoses and connectors and make sure that these are free. Sometimes a cigarette butt can clog a hose and allow all sorts of dirt to become trapped in the hose ahead of it, thus building a "dam" that will block the passage of additional air. If you have made all these checks and the motor still seems to be operating, yet no air is being pulled in, by all means check to see that the back cover plate is properly in position and is not blowing wind. Some vacuums offer an accessory plate that can be removed so that the vacuum can act as a compressor for blowing air into a paint sprayer. If this plate is opened, the machine won't work.

The next task is to open the unit so that you can visually inspect the motor and fan. We've run into this problem more than once: the small set screws that hold the fan to the motor shaft have loosened, so that while the motor is turning properly, the fan just sits there. To correct this situation, tighten the screws but make sure that the fan is not hitting any internal obstructions.

You may find a semi-mechanical problem in the form of a motor that has seized. What happens is that the motor will be so in need of lubrication that it heats up and the shaft cannot turn. Once you have established that this is the problem, turn off the machine and allow it to cool, then try to rotate the shaft of the motor manually. If it does turn, apply some oil to the proper places (the little holes marked "oil") and rotate the shaft until it turns easily.

If you have a burned-out motor, it can be repaired. Bring it to a motor service shop, where they are equipped to rewind the coils and replace the entire coil with a new one. They will then test the motor and return it to you in like-new condition.

The motor service shop, however, will want you to completely dismount the motor from the cleaner. This is not difficult. Locate the motor's shaft and unscrew the two set screws that hold the fan blades to the shaft. At the bottom of some units you'll find what is called the motor "pad," which is a base through which screws will pass into the vacuum's housing. Remove these screws and the motor should sit loosely in place. Locate the two wires that go from the switch to the motor, disconnect them, and the motor should lift out easily.

Other units use long bolts set into the end bell of the motor housing instead of a pad or base arrangement. Loosen these screws in like fashion to dismount the motor.

Electrical problems other than those directly concerning the motor are far easier to contend with. You may, for example, find that the power cord has frayed and isn't providing proper voltage to the motor. You can easily correct this by removing the plug, undoing the connection to the motor, and then shortening the cord to remove the frayed portion. Reestablish the connection and you should be back in business.

The on-off switch can also go sour and might even evidence this failure by not operating properly. It will flop loosely up and down without turning anything on. Many vacuum cleaners are equipped with a simple two-position on-off switch. If the switch is a standard one, it will be equipped with a half-inch mounting shaft, held in place by a half-inch hex nut. Remove the top portion of the vacuum cleaner's handle, remove the nut, and pull out the bad switch. Snake the wires through the hole, put a replacement switch in (any electronic store has these) and wire it into place. Replace the nut, and you're all set.

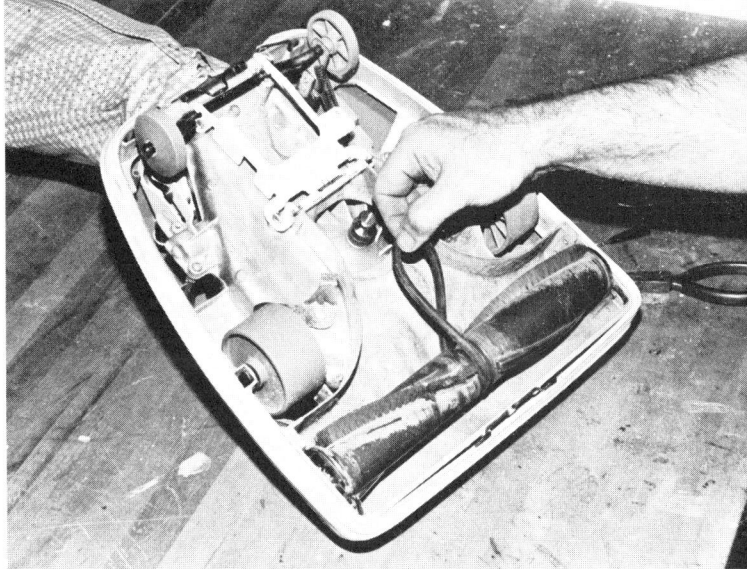

Next, put the new belt in place, re-install the beater roll, and slip the belt over the small pulley.

Put back the cover plate.

Now that operation is completed.

To replace a broken drive belt, first upend the machine and simply lift the beater out of its mounts.

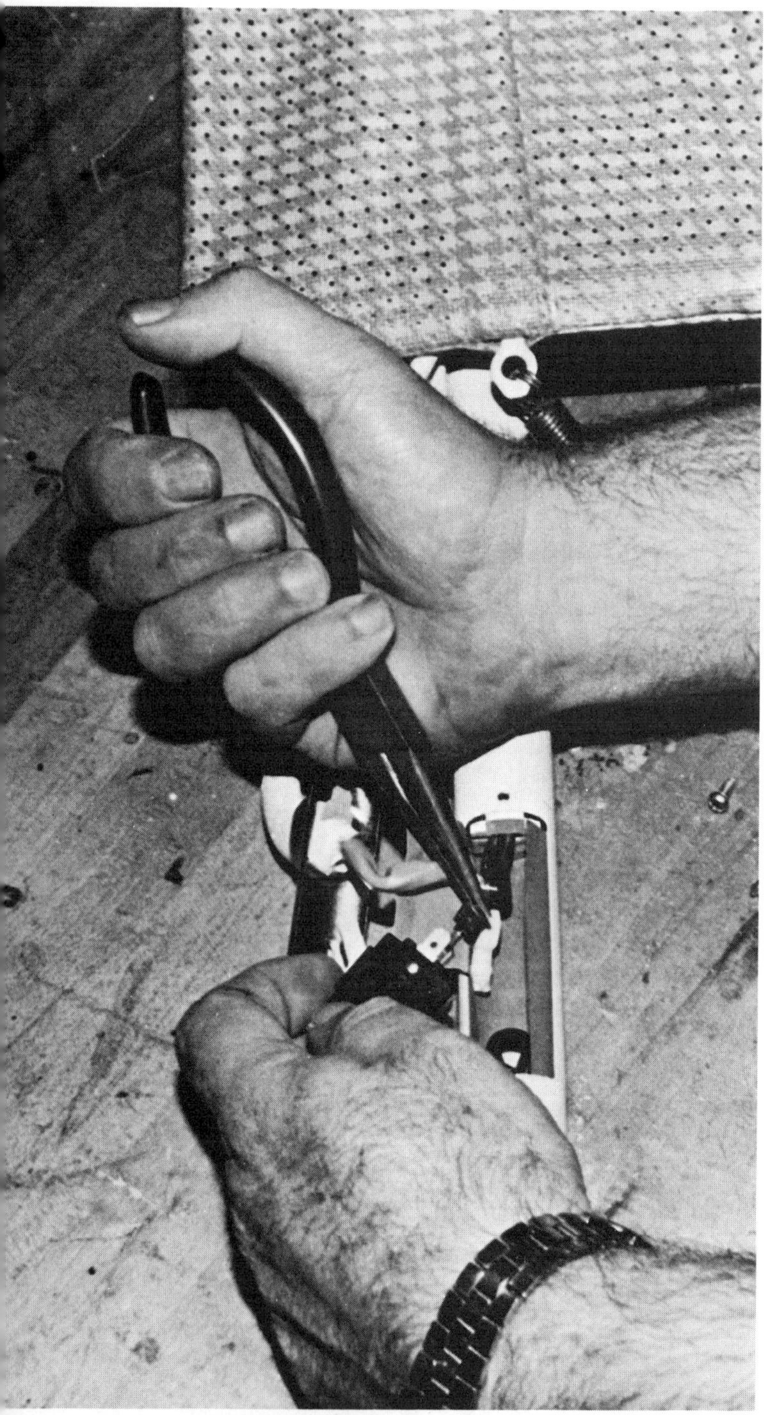

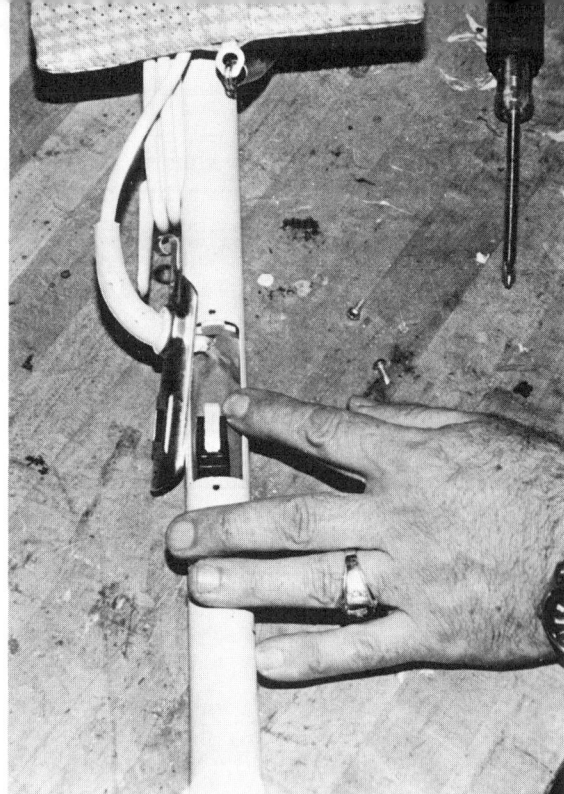

Then put heavy insulating paper back in place.

Finally, the plate is put back and the screws tightened.

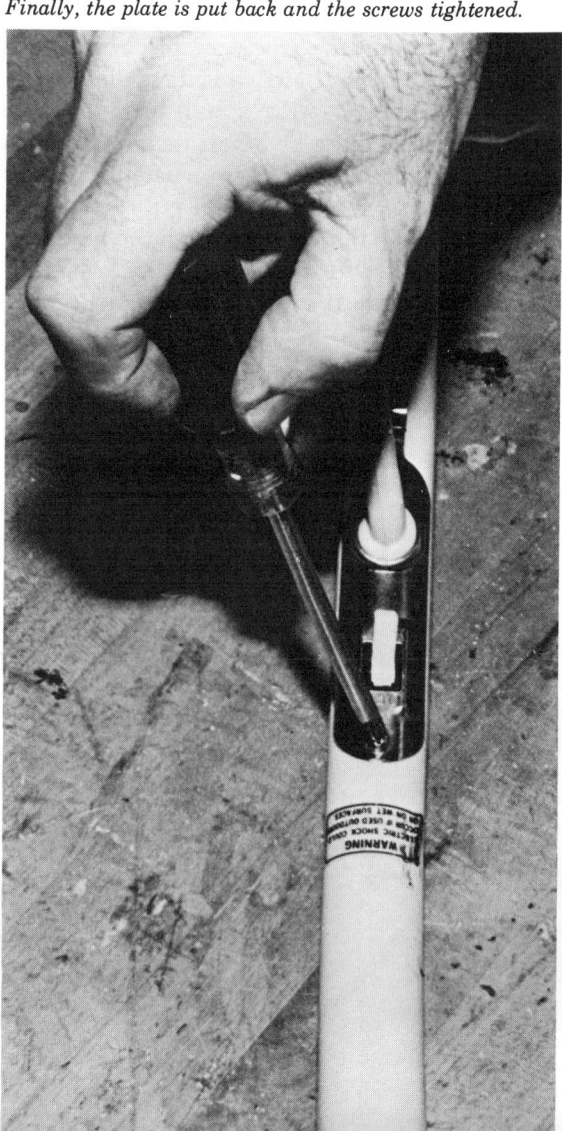

If the switch is not working, first remove switch plate, and install new switch.

13
Blenders

Blenders can fail for a number of reasons, but the most common electrical failure is caused by people who don't know how to use the blender. It's another case of assuming knowledge you do not possess.

Users know, for example, that they can quickly and easily grind potatoes in the blender, but how many users realize that you must dice the potatoes first? They cut the potato into large chunks and toss the chunks into the blender hoping that the blender can handle them. Because the potato has *not* been cut into half-inch cubes first, the blender overworks and the motor overheats. If the motor overheats sufficiently, it burns out.

Another of the ills the blender is subject to concerns its use in attempting to puree solids without adding sufficient liquids. The blender does require that liquids be added in order for it to do its best work, and if you do not add sufficient liquid, the blender will bind and overheat.

Finally, people simply will not understand that once the blending process is complete, there is no advantage in keeping the machine running. They mix a drink, for example, and the poor blender is left running long after the drink is thoroughly blended. Never allow the blender to run for protracted periods of time.

Other situations may arise. The blender makes a good summer drink by chopping ice cubes into slush. Add some sweet flavoring and you've got an excellent summer treat. But can you imagine what those hard ice cubes do to the blades? Do this sort of thing often enough, and you're going to have to sharpen or hone the blades occasionally. Sometimes too, liquids will overflow, get into the electronic controlling mechanism, and dampen the circuitry. But we are concerned with repair. Let's see what can be done when it needs doing.

If the blade is in need of honing, remove the blade completely from the unit by loosening and removing the holding nuts. You can use a carbide-type scissors sharpener to best advantage here. Make sure you observe the orientation of the blade when replacing it.

If the motor has overheated and stopped, don't begin ripping the housing apart yet. Many of these motors are fitted with thermal cutouts that are designed to break the circuit and stop the motor if it should overheat. If this sort of thing does happen, all you have to do is wait a while until the motor has

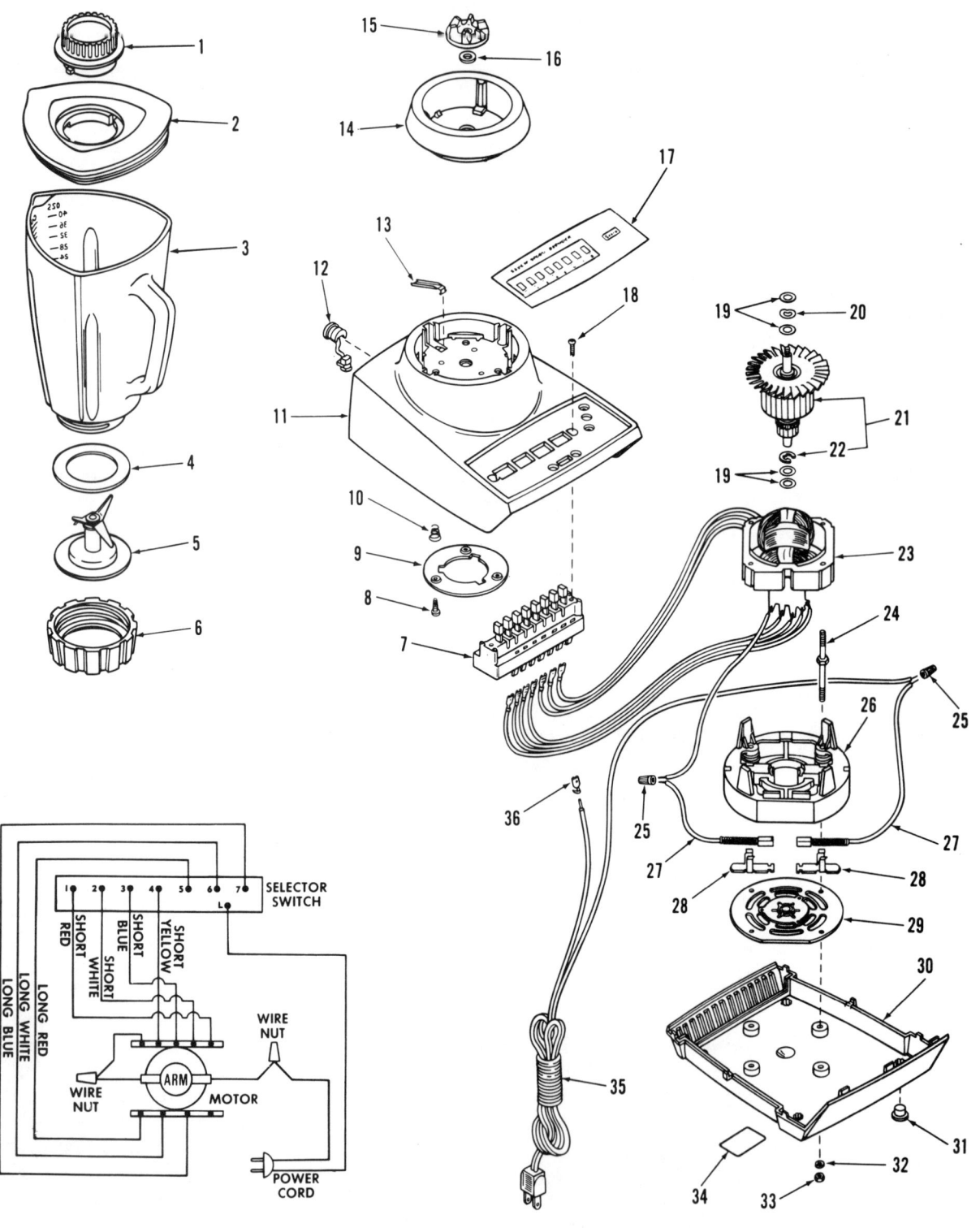

Parts illustrations for modern blender. Courtesy of Sears, Roebuck and Co.

36   Small Appliance Repair

REPAIR PARTS LIST

Key No.	Description
1	Fill Cap
2	Container Cover
2	Container Cover
3	Container
4	Gasket
5	Cutting Unit
6	Container Base
6	Container Base
7	Switch
8	*Screw (3 used) #6-20 x 5/16 in. Phillips type 25 Thread Cutting
9	Baffle Plate
10	Spring (3 used)
11	Upper Housing Assy.
11	Upper Housing Assy.
12	Strain Relief
13	Drain
14	Self Centering Ring
15	Clutch
16	*Washer 1/2 in. O.D. x .252 Hole x .032 Thk S. Steel
17	Switch Plate - Moss Green
17	Switch Plate - Saddle Tan
18	*Screw (2 used) #6-20 x 1/2 in. Phillips type 25 Thread Cutting
19	*Washer (4 used) 1/2 in. O.D. x .322 Hole x .015 Thk. Steel
20	*Spring Washer .492 O.D. x .327 Hole x .005 Thk. Steel
21	Armature W/Retaining Ring
22	Retaining Ring
23	Field
24	Field Stud (4 used)
25	Wire Nut (2 used)
26	Brush Holder Housing
27	Brush & Spring Set
28	Brush Cap (2 used)
29	Motor Cap Complete
30	Lower Housing
31	Bumper (4 used)
32	*Lockwasher (4 used) #8 Screw .047 x .031
33	*Nut (4 used) 8-32 x 1/4 in. Hex 3/32 in. Thk. Steel
34	Nomenclature Insert
35	Cord
36	Terminal

*Standard Hardware item, may be purchased locally.

Courtesy of Sears, Roebuck and Co.

cooled sufficiently and the unit will operate as well as ever.

Most modern blenders are controlled by electronic circuits. These circuits, in turn, are controlled by switches that select the necessary components to operate the blender at the desired speed. The motor of most blenders is a voltage-sensitive device that will vary in speed with variations in voltage. The several switches can select the correct circuit to provide the necessary voltage that will control the speed to the desired amount. This action can also be provided by a series of diodes, which are electronic devices that accomplish the same effect with more control and efficiency.

If your blender is not working properly, determine which cycles are operating correctly and which are not by operating the various switches and observing the action. If the unit fails to function correctly on one or more of the switches, disassemble the control circuit after unplugging the blender and expose the electronic circuitry. If resistors are used and one or more are burned open, they will be obvious by the discoloration. If diodes are used, they will have to be unsoldered from the circuit and tested.

Blenders are supposed to be operated cyclically, that is, on and off. If the blender has been exposed to a continuous and heavy load, the electronic components can indeed burn open. Unfortunately, resistors, once overheated, will change in value and you cannot measure the resistance (which might no longer be correct) and substitute a new one. You must find out what the original value was. Again, unfortunately, once a resistor has overheated, the color bands that denote its value will alter as well.

The only thing you can do is call the local authorized service representative and ask what the correct value of resistance was originally intended to be. Obtain a replacement resistor of at least the same wattage rating and the exact same resistance value and solder the replacement into the control unit in the same place.

If diodes were used, these can be tested by unsoldering them from the circuit and using your ohmmeter. Start by placing the ohmmeter leads on the diode leads and note the value indicated on your meter. Now reverse the meter leads and again check the reading. If a diode is operating correctly, you should have a high reading in one direction and a low reading in the reverse.

When replacing a diode, note the polarity, or direction in which the diode must be connected. Usually, there is a small spot of paint on one end of the diode, or a small symbol (   ) printed on the body of the diode to indicate polarity. The new one must be replaced in the same "direction" as the one you removed.

Incidentally, heat can damage a diode too. When you're soldering the new diode into place, always clamp a heat sink between the point you are soldering and the body of the diode to leech the heat away from the unit.

To help you in replacing these units, here's a method you can use: Instead of unsoldering the bad part, clip it out with your wire cutter and leave a length of the old lead extended. Now twist the lead wires of the new unit into small five-turn spirals, using another piece of wire as a form. Clip away the excess. Now slip the spiral over the excess lead you left, crimp it with your pliers, and solder it into position.

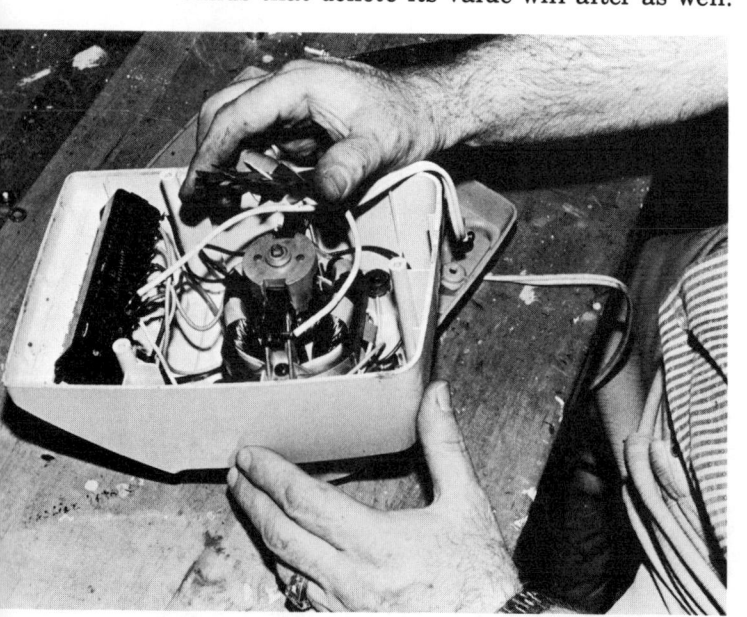

Unscrew the nut that holds the fan in place under the blender.

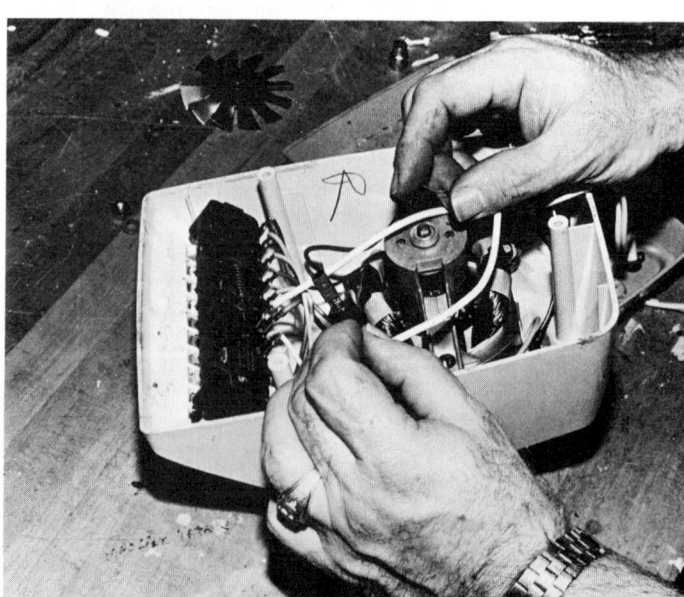

Note that with the mounting clip removed, the brushes slide out for easy replacement.

Disconnecting the circuit element is simply a matter of sliding the wiring clips off the contacts. Note which color wire goes to which terminal, however.

14
Electric Shavers

First turn the switch to "on," with the shaver head removed to take away any load. If the motor seems to be operating normally with the head removed, the problem might well be in the head itself. If the motor does not operate, try turning it with your fingers (unplug the unit first) to see if it turns freely. If it does, check the input connections to the motor to make sure that it is getting electricity. If it is not, check to see that the switch is operating. All you might have to do is to burnish the "goo" from the switch contacts with a small brush to restore the shaver to operation. Once you've got the motor operating, check one more thing. Some shavers are equipped with a knurled knob attached to the shaft. You flip this knob with your finger to start the motor, and this is normal operation for that type of motor.

If the motor operates with the head removed but does not operate with the head in place, do the following. Take the head apart and clean it thoroughly, working on a clean, lint-free surface, and mark each part as you disassemble it. Clean all the parts in alcohol and allow them to air dry. Apply a drop of light oil as you reassemble the unit. If you are unable to get electric shaver oil, you can substitute light typewriter oil which we've found works even better as it won't gum up or sludge in time.

Sharpening these oscillating-type shavers, in which the blade slides back and forth under the cutting head, can be very tricky and if you are faced with what is obviously a dull blade, consider replacing the blade element entirely.

On the other hand, you may have one of the Norelco-type shavers which have rotating blades in sets of one-, two-, or three-head models that float to conform to your facial features. The biggest problem with these is that the blades are lapped to the blade guards. If you ever have occasion to take the blade out of the guard, make sure that you put the same blade back into the same guard! You should also know that there is a special sharpening tool available for this type of razor, consisting of a fine honing stone mounted in a plastic handle. To use it, you open the shaver head, hold the stone over the blade, and turn on the razor. This stone proceeds to strop the blade the same way the barber strops his straight razor in his shop. You begin to get sharp, clean shaves once again.

Cleaning the razor is the best preventive maintenance you can apply. After each shave, open the razor head and use the small brush that came with the razor to get rid of all the pulverized hairs. Because we use various pre- and after-shave lotions and skin conditioners, these fine pieces of hair can become coated with the various chemicals and will soon pack and gum the razor. The hairs are visible, however, and you will know when the razor is properly cleaned. We suggest using the brush daily. Once a week take the razor's head off and give it a thorough going-over. This should include a soaking cleaning with alcohol.

If the head guard or blade guard becomes bent or dented, do not try to use the razor until after this has been straightened out or replaced, because the indentation will only serve to dull the blades. If you try to straighten this yourself and push it too far in the wrong direction, the razor will pull instead of cutting.

Always check the line cord too, to be sure that it isn't frayed or worn to the point where wire is exposed. If it is, always buy a new exact replacement cord rather than try to make do. (We've seen people try to jam a TV cheater cord into the razor's socket. All you can do is cause additional damage.)

Depending on the type of electric razor, there are additional repairs you can make that will restore like-new operation.

Electric razors of the rotary-head type have the blade edges actually lapped or honed to the protective guard surface. People who do not take the trouble to read the accompanying instruction booklet might take the razor apart for cleaning and replace the blades under different guard surfaces. This will happen when you have a multi-headed razor: you remove the two or three rotary blades and put them back in incorrect sequence.

The razor will work, but it will not work as it once did, with the most comfort and efficiency. The procedure here is to replace the blades and shaver head, but you can take steps to correct this yourself. Your local automotive supply dealer can provide you with a very fine valve grinding compound. Apply this liberally to the undersurfaces of the guards, then reassemble the unit and turn the razor on for a second or two. Next, carefully remove all of the compound and clean the razor thoroughly. You will have corrected any mismatch and the razor's performance should improve considerably.

15
Air Fresheners and Humidifiers

Essentially, the humidifier consists of a tank of water through which an endless belt of absorbent material passes. Usually, a foam plastic belt is used. As the belt passes through the water, a fan blows air through the belt and into the room. The belt not only carries the water, it serves as an air filter as well. Controls on the unit adjust the speed at which the belt passes through the water, and the speed at which the fan operates.

What can go wrong with these units? Several things. The most common complaint is that the foam plastic belt stretches, forms additional loops, and binds around its own rollers. If this happens, remove the entire mechanism and free the belt. You will find that the belt is not formed in one piece but rather is butted against its own ends and secured, either by a cement, a tape, or even staples. Cut away the joint and reattach the belt to remove the slack. Reassemble the entire unit and the belt should operate satisfactorily again.

Some of the better-quality units have a float inside that is attached to a leaf switch. The function of this switch is to cut off the power if the water in the tank falls below a certain level. On units that are permanently connected to a water line, you may find that a float switch and valve are used to refill the tank automatically as it empties. Make sure that the float and the switch are operating correctly.

The belt speed control is usually a variable resistive-type unit that, because of the constant exposure to moisture, may oxidize. Should sufficient oxidation build up, the wiper arm will no longer make contact. The same thing can happen with the fan speed switch, which is usually a rotary type with several positions. You may find that the fan works at certain speeds, but not at others. This is a good indication that oxidation has occurred.

To correct this situation, obtain television switch cleaner and spray this liberally on the controls. Work the controls rapidly to remove the oxidation. If this corrects the problem for you, the following steps will keep it from happening again.

Form a small sack of porous muslin, cotton, or cheesecloth and fill the sack with mothballs. Hang this inside the unit. Mothballs keep oxides from forming on silver (the switch contacts are silver).

The difference between an air freshener and a humidifier is a matter of scent. You can add any water-soluble odor, such as pine, and fill the room with a freshness that was not there before.

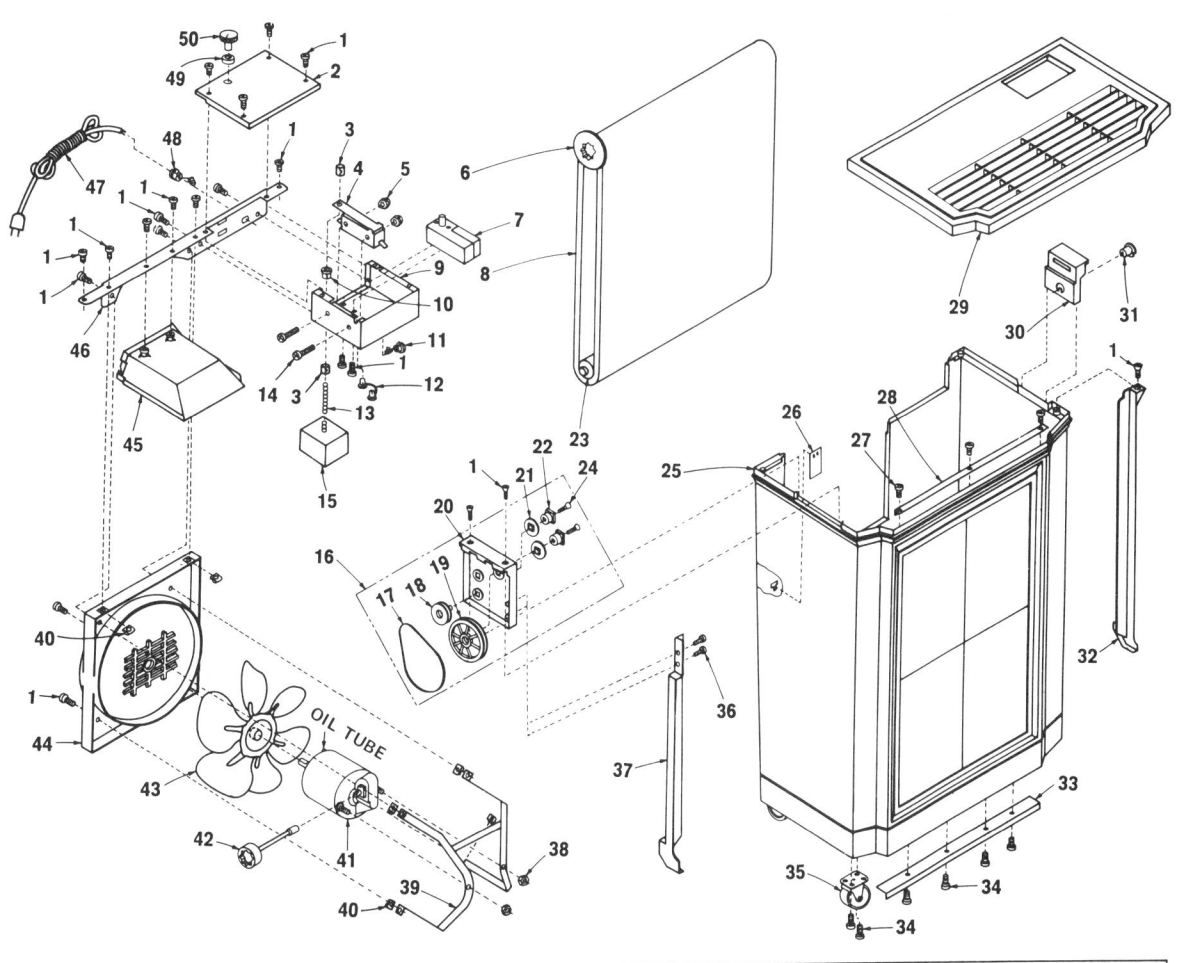

KEY NO.	DESCRIPTION	KEY NO.	DESCRIPTION
1	*Screw, #8 x 1/2" Phillips Pan Head, Type-AB	27	*Screw, #6-32 x 3/8" Phillips Pan Head, Type-D
2	Nameplate	28	Brace
3	Nut	29	Lid
4	Switch	30	Bracket, Bearing
5	*Nut, Hex #6-32	31	Bearing, Roller
6	Roller, Drive	32	Channel
7	Humidistat	33	Brace, Bottom
8	Roto-Belt™	34	*Screw, #10-24 x 1/2" Phillips Pan Head, Type-D
9	Box, Switch	35	Caster
10	Bushing	36	*Screw, #8-32 x 3/8" Phillips Pan Head, Type-D
11	Bushing		
12	Clamp	37	Channel
13	Chain	38	*Nut, Lock #8-32
14	*Screw, #6-32 x 1" Phillips Pan Head, Machine	39	Support
		40	*Nut (For #8 Sheet Metal Screw)
15	Float	41	Motor
16	Box Assembly, Drive	42	Shaft
17	Belt	43	Blade, Fan
18	Pulley	44	Grill
19	Pulley	45	Shield
20	Box, Drive	46	Support
21	Bearing	47	Cord Kit
22	Bracket, Drive	48	Bushing
23	Roller, Idler	49	Washer
24	Screw, #4 x 3/8" Phillips Flat Head, Type-T	50	Knob
25	Housing		
26	Indicator		

*Standard Hardware Item — May Be Purchased Locally.

Courtesy of Sears, Roebuck and Co.

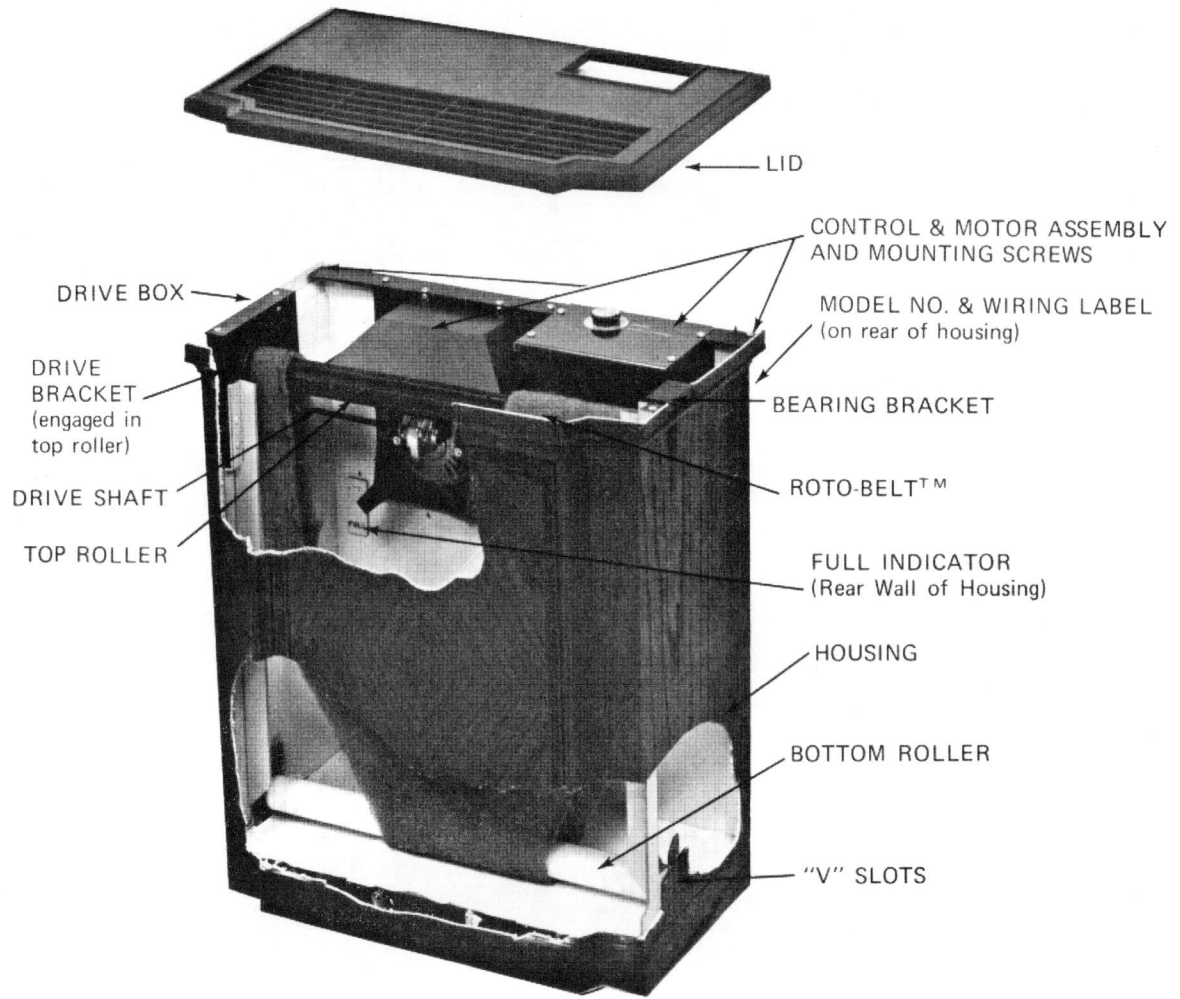

Courtesy of Sears, Roebuck and Co. *Parts replacement for a humidifier.*

16
Electric Blankets

The biggest problem in servicing will not be in the blanket itself, but rather, in the control unit. If the wiring or heating unit in the blanket goes bad, replace the blanket — do not try to repair it, for it's virtually impossible.

Repairs of the control unit are not difficult. However, if the blanket does not get warm, first you have to ascertain that the problem is, indeed, in the control and not in the blanket. Do this by taking a continuity check on the blanket terminals. You should get high resistance continuity through the wiring.

The problem is: how do you get into the control unit to service it? On one unit we examined a small sheet-metal screw was visible on the bottom plate. We removed that and the plate came off, yet the unit still did not come apart. We removed a part of the wood-grained decorative covering, which turned out to be ordinary Contact paper revealing two sheet-metal screws at the bottom. We removed those and still the unit did not separate into what was obviously two halves of the plastic housing. We removed the rest of the wood-grained paper and found that all that held the two halves together at that point was the paper.

A four-position slider switch was used to set the basic temperature level, with a small neon lamp to indicate "On." The unit is heftily constructed and uses a wire-wound resistor for control purposes. Presumably, a surge of power might knock out this unit, but that isn't likely. If such a surge were to occur, chances are that other appliances in your own home and in your neighbors' homes would also suffer as a result.

A thermostat with a variable setting controls the on-and-off action of this device. This is a hot-wire thermostat that is spot-welded at the distal end to the thermostatic spring. Under this spring are the contacts.

Begin by checking the hot wire and the spring to make sure that they are still fastened. It is possible that the weld could break, in which case it needs to be rewelded. You might conceivably be able to solder this, but its own heat would destory the connection. Any well-equipped welding shop can reweld this for you for a modest charge.

Check the unit in operation with the control box open. If the thermostat opens and closes with changes in the control setting, unplug the unit and use ordinary brown wrapping paper or bag paper to clean the contacts. Slip the paper under the open contact, press down the contact with your finger; then, while holding down the contact, pull out the paper. If you see any signs or traces of oxides, repeat this until the paper comes out clean. In case of a large buildup of oxidation on the contacts, obtain some liquid contact cleaner and some small cotton swabs and do a thorough job of cleaning. These contacts are usually of coin silver, and if oxidation is the problem, the circuit will work but the oxides will not allow contact to be made. To prevent — or at least reduce — the buildup of oxides in the future, find a place in the housing where you can drop a mothball. (Mothballs are made of paradichlorobenzene, which inhibits the formation of oxides on silver surfaces.) Put the mothball into the housing, button it up, and you're back in business.

Now to reassemble the control unit. We had no problem in putting the unit together and getting the screws back into place, but the woodgrained Contact paper was shot. We bought some new Contact and used a simple trick to replace it.

Remove the old paper completely, and use it as a pattern to cut the new paper to size. Now mix up a large bowl of liquid detergent and water, using only a few drops of the detergent. (The proportions are not critical.) Remove the backing paper from the Contact and dip the Contact into the water/detergent mixture. Coat the adhesive side completely. Now put the Contact into place. Slide it around until it's where you want it, press it down, and let it sit for an hour or so until it dries. Press it down once again, and it will adhere. If there are small air bubbles, puncture these with a pin and press the air out of them.

17
Electric Pencil Sharpeners

While there are many types of pencil sharpeners, both electric-power operated and battery-operated, they still fall into two groups, determined by the blade arrangement. Less expensive units use a single blade held in a tapered block, much like the old pencil sharpeners that came with your pencil box when you were a youngster. The better-grade units have two cylindrical structures mounted at an angle. The two cylinders are laced with spiral-grooved blades, and the cylinders counter-rotate on a geared mechanism to put a point on the pencil.

Whether battery- or AC-powered, many of the units have nice accessory features. The on-off cycling is controlled by the pencil itself, so that when a pencil is inserted into the sharpener, it begins to work, and stops when the pencil is removed. Some units are also equipped with three small lamps that are operated by switches inside the unit. The lamps are fitted with colored gels that light up progressively to indicate to the user just how sharp a point is placed on the pencil. If you want a sharp point, keep pressing the pencil in until the last lamp comes on.

Generally, these units are simple and little can go wrong with them. However, the totally foolproof machine has not yet been invented, so let's see what possible defects there are and how we can correct them.

Usually, as long as the motor operates, the unit will function properly, but the shavings drawer *must* be emptied periodically. If the drawer has not been emptied and the unit has been in constant use, the shavings will compact and can cause trouble by jamming the works. Begin by checking to see that the drawer is emptied and that all shavings have been removed from the blade area or the rotating mechanism. Apply some light lubricant to all rotating parts.

If this does not correct the problem, check with your voltmeter to see that proper voltage is being delivered to the motor itself. If it is and if the motor does not work, you may have a burned-out motor. If this occurs, you can replace the motor — provided an exact duplicate can be located.

If proper voltage is not being delivered to the motor, but the unit is properly connected to a voltage source, check at the input to the switch to see if the switch is getting voltage. You will find either that you have a faulty switch or that the switch-operating lever or tab has taken a "set" and must be readjusted. You can adjust the tab with long-nose pliers, but make certain that you disconnect the unit while making such an adjustment.

It is highly unlikely that the edge on your blade will not outlast the other components, but it could happen. If your blades are of the multiple cylindrical variety, the sharpening process is an involved one that we do not advise you to attempt to repair. However, if it is a single-blade rotary type, you can remove the blade by loosening a single screw. Hone the blade properly on a whetstone, then replace the blade in its plastic block. You will observe that the screw-mounting hole in the blade is slotted, so that you can adjust the blade easily. We recommended that you begin by inserting a sharpened pencil all the way into the sharpener and loosen the mounting screw so that the blade edge rests lightly on the sharpened portion of the pencil. Tighten the screw and try the unit. If it seems to be hogging too much wood at a time, back off the blade. If it does not sharpen properly or sufficiently, move the blade downward, always using your well-sharpened pencil as a guide to assure the proper blade angle.

To hone the blade properly, you will note that one side of the blade is bevelled to a sharp edge. Hold this bevel against your stone and hone the edge in a circular motion. After several strokes in this fashion, invert the blade, laying the back of it flat on the stone, and repeat the movement to remove any burrs.

Always test these units before reassembling them into the housings. If further adjustment is needed, you can save time by this testing so you won't have to strip the unit down again.

A special switch is mounted at the rear of the sharpening blades, inside the unit. This is a pressure-sensitive switching mechanism that activates the motor as soon as a pencil is inserted, starting the shaving process that points the pencil.

When the pencil is sharp enough to apply pressure on the first of an additional three positions, an indicator lamp lights up. As the pencil becomes sharper, it can penetrate deeper into the pencil socket, causing the second lamp and then the third lamp to light.

If one or more of the lamps do not light, the probability is that the lamp requires replacing. Invert the unit and remove the holding screws that will release the top lid and provide accesss to the lamps. Depending upon the unit, the lamps might require soldering to replace them, but more often they are of the telephone type that simply slide into their sockets. To remove the old lamp and check that it is indeed burned open, place a bit of pressure-sensitive tape over the glass portion and, pulling on the tape, slide the lamp out. Without the tape or a special tool, getting the lamp out can be a problem, as the lamps are difficult to grip with bare fingers.

Substitute the lamp for one that has been working in the unit. If it fails to work in a socket known to be good, you've got to substitute a new lamp. If new lamps do not work, the problem might well be in the switching mechanism, which must be replaced completely by a new unit that you can obtain from an authorized service facility. Remove the old switch and replace it with the new one, resoldering the connections.

Some units are battery-powered, and the first corrective step, if batteries are used, is to replace the old battery with a new one.

If the unit operates on alternating current, make certain that it is getting the proper voltage at the motor by plugging the unit in, inserting a pencil, and placing your voltmeter test prods at the motor terminals. If no voltage is present, check the outlet to see that it is functioning properly.

18
Phonographs/Stereos

If the entire unit seems dead — no sound at all, the motor doesn't rotate the turntable, the indicator lamps, if any, do not come on — you should determine that the unit is properly plugged in and that voltage is getting to the system. Next, check to find a fuse on the unit itself. This may appear on a rear skirt of the phono and look like a small black knob that you can twist off. A small glass cartridge-type fuse will come away with the knob. Check the fuse with your ohmmeter and if it is not continuous, replace the fuse with an exact duplicate.

If the motor operates the turntable but you get no amplification, check to see if it is a tube-type set. If it is, draw a position map of the various tube locations, remove the tubes, and have them tested. You will probably find one or more aren't functioning; replacing them will restore the unit to operation.

If you get sound out of one speaker in a stereo system but not out of the other, first check the position of the balance control. If it is properly centered, try disconnecting the wires that plug in from the phono to the amplifier and see if the sound now comes out of the other speaker. This may indicate that you have either a faulty amplifier or a faulty connecting wire, which you can easily replace by purchasing a new one at any electronic supply house.

If you're getting muddy sound, the fault might lie either in your cartridge or the stylus. Remove the cartridge from the tone arm, taking care not to touch the stylus. Bring the cartridge (together with the stylus) to any local hi-fi service shop where the stylus can be examined under a microscope for wear. If sufficient wear is evident, you will want to replace the stylus. For some unknown reason, people like to run a finger over the stylus to see if things are "working." It's a good way to destroy a stylus and the resulting sound is almost a profanity in itself.

You can help isolate faults in a phonograph if it has more than one input. If the unit is a combination record player/radio receiver, by all means check to see if the other portion functions when one portion fails.

If you have what is called a record changer, you might find after a while that the change cycle is very slow. This can be caused by having too many records on the turntable or by a lack of lubrication underneath (where it counts). Begin by removing the record changer from the cabinet and up-end it over a pile of newspapers. Lubricate all moving parts generously, but avoid lubrication on rubber parts. This treatment should help the situation, but if you still find things binding a bit, turn the unit over so that the turntable is facing up. At the center of the spindle, you'll find a small split "C" clip. Put the point of a small screwdriver at the middle of the "C" and press.

With the C-washer removed, carefully lift the turntable itself, freeing it of the rim-drive mechanism. Lift the turntable off the spindle, just as though it were a record. This will expose the inner workings hidden under the turntable. Apply lubrication to all moving parts; where metal bears on metal use some light, white grease.

Reassemble the turntable to the mechanism, seat the driving device properly, and then carefully replace the C-washer.

The phonograph is a delicate electronic device, and you should avoid any attempt to repair the electronic circuitry. This is not an area that the do-it-yourselfer should attempt to fix unless he has specific electronic knowledge of servicing techniques.

19
Electric Lamps

Many things can go wrong with lamps. The switch in the socket can go sour and will have to be replaced, the line cord can fray and short circuit, or the various components holding the lamp together can work loose.

If the switch or socket shows evidence of failure, you are best advised to replace the entire socket. Sometimes you can even save that part of the job. Let's begin by taking the bulb out and removing the plug from the wall outlet.

Look down into the socket and you will see a small, phosphor-bronze spring that makes contact with the tip connector on the base of the light bulb. Reach in and get a fingernail under that bronze contact. Now lift it slightly so that it leans upward at more of an angle. Often, the pressure of the bulb will cause this contact to take a "set" so that it no longer contacts the lamp base. Pulling it up slightly can correct the problem.

If this has not helped, visit your local lumber yard and buy a new socket. If you look around the side of the socket, you will see the word "Press." Press at that point with your finger and the socket will pull apart easily in your hand. Unscrew the two screw terminals and remove the wires, assemble the new socket in place and reconnect the wires to the screws. Then reassemble the socket by pressing the brass shell cover over the fiber inner shell and back into the metal outer cap. Screw the new socket back over the threaded center rod of the lamp, put the bulb in, plug it in, and it should light up.

Should the lamp components seem loose or wobbly begin by unplugging the lamp, and then turn it on its side. Look at the base of the lamp. You'll generally find a felt base. Strip this felt away, which exposes the innards of the lamp base. You'll see the lower end of the center-threaded rod with the wire coming out of it. Use a large pair of pliers and carefully tighten the hexagonal screw that holds this rod in place. Make it good and tight, and then adjust all of the lamp's components to be sure they are in proper alignment. In doing so, you may make a little added slack in the threaded rod and you can take this up by tightening the nut once again.

While you're in the base of the lamp, also inspect the power cord. Frequently, this will get all twisted up and now is your chance to straighten it out, or even replace the cord entirely with a new one.

When you have finished this operation, cut a heavy piece of felt to the size of

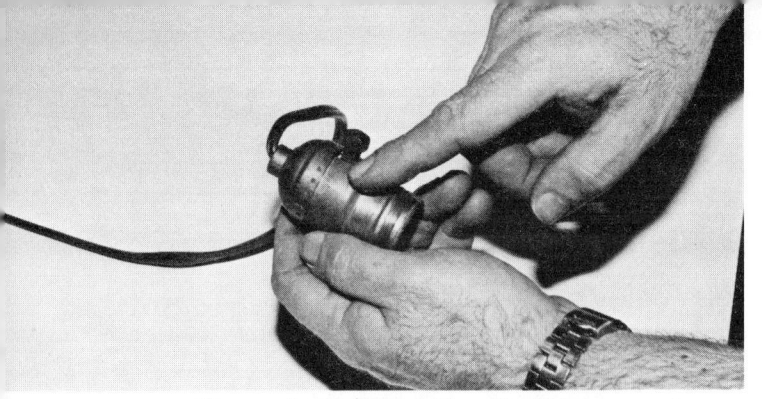

Finger points to the word "press" which is stamped on every socket.

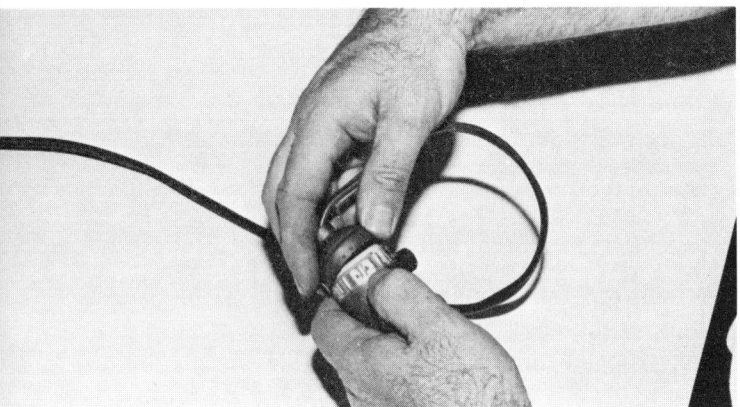

By pressing you release the top of the socket cap. Remove this and slide along the wire.

With the cap off you can remove the brass cover, the cardboard insulating sleeve, and the old wiring from the socket terminals.

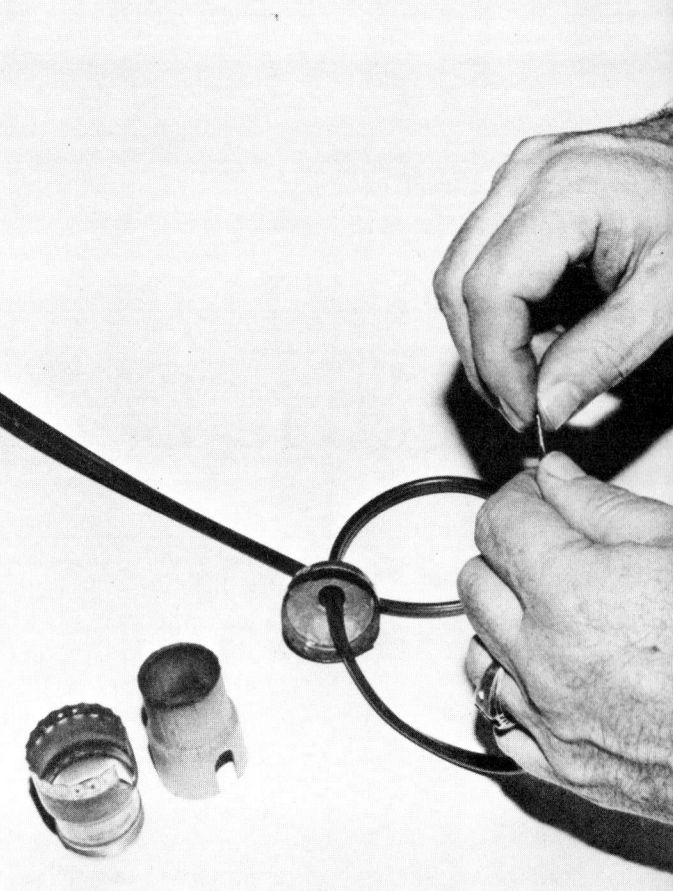

Slip the new wiring into the cap of the new socket. Strip and twist the ends of the wire.

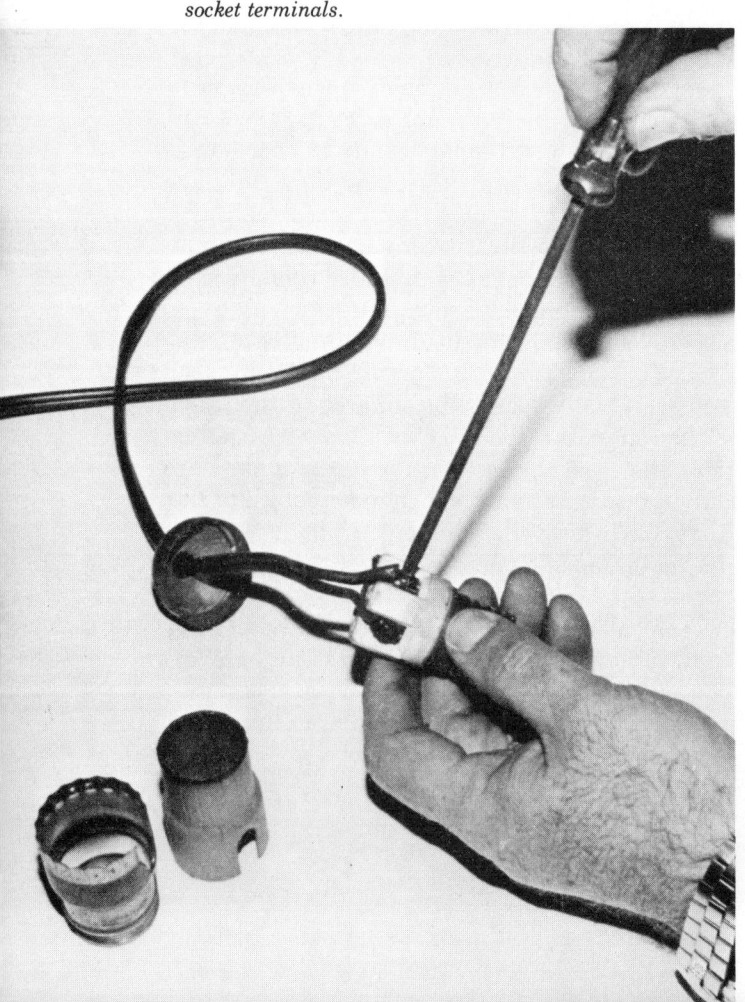

the base, and cement it in place with some ordinary mucilage so that the base of the lamp will glide easily on your furniture.

At the other end of the lamp cord is the plug that goes into the wall outlet. Check it carefully. If it is showing any signs of wear, replace it with a new one. Cut the old one off and expose the two separate wires coming from the lamp. Separate about two inches of this, tie a U.L. knot, and then strip about half an inch of the insulation from each of the wires. Twist the strands of each wire together and then run the wires clockwise around the plug screw connectors, tightening the screws. There are certain types of plugs you merely insert the wire into without stripping. Pushing a lever down makes contact and the plug is ready to use.

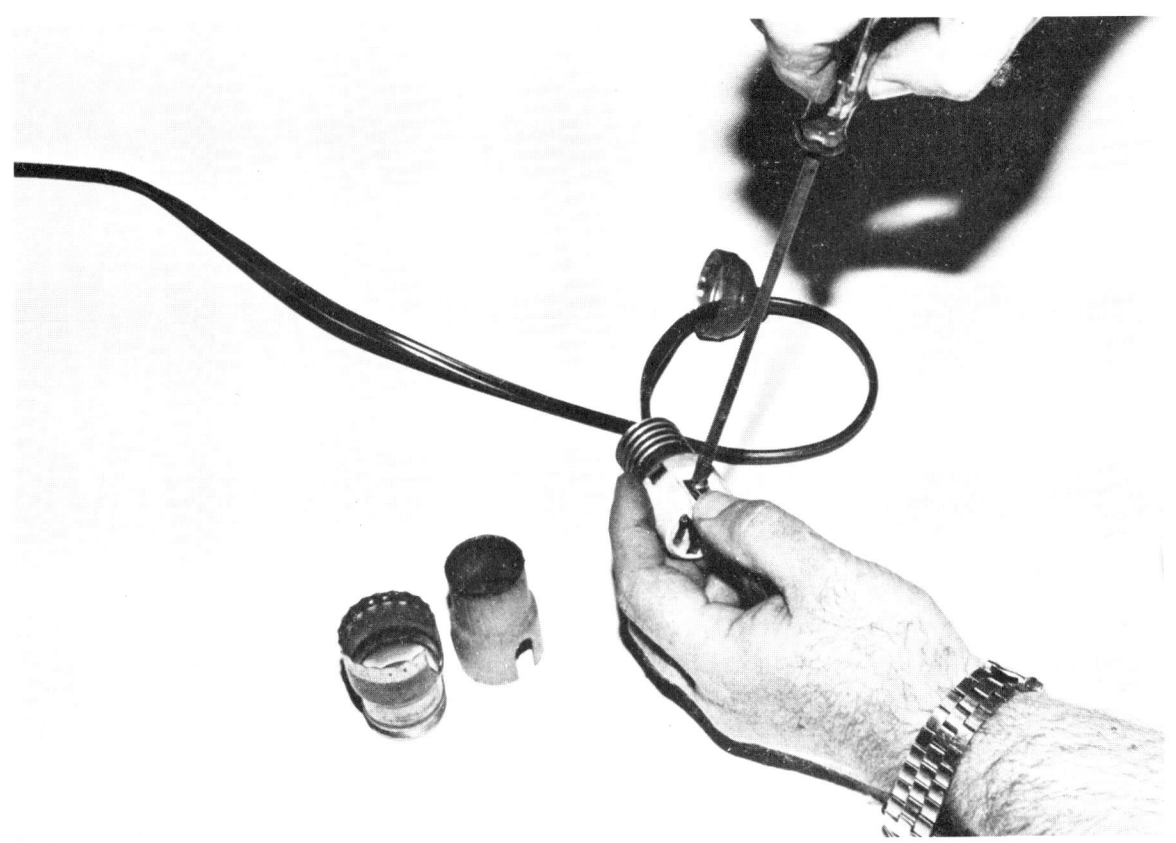

Connect the new wire to the terminals.

Pop the brass cover back in place and you are now ready to reassemble the new socket to the lamp.

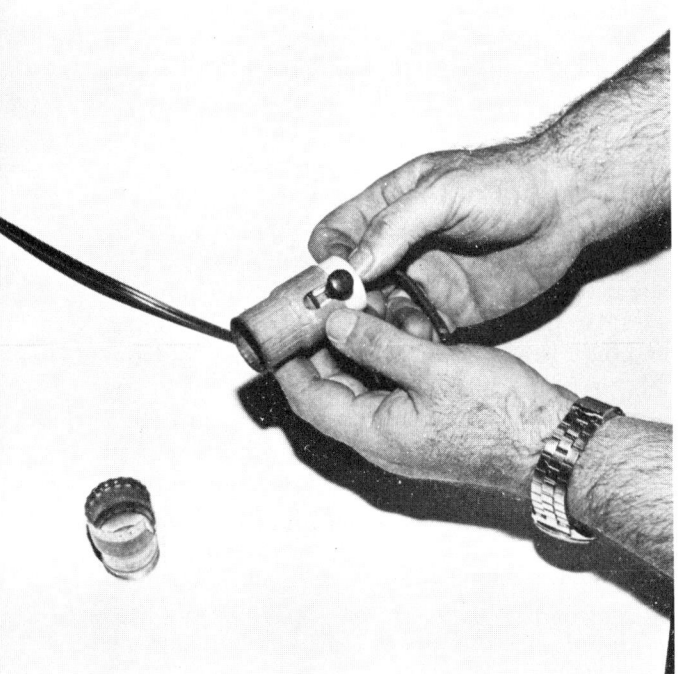

Then slip the cardboard sleeve over the socket.

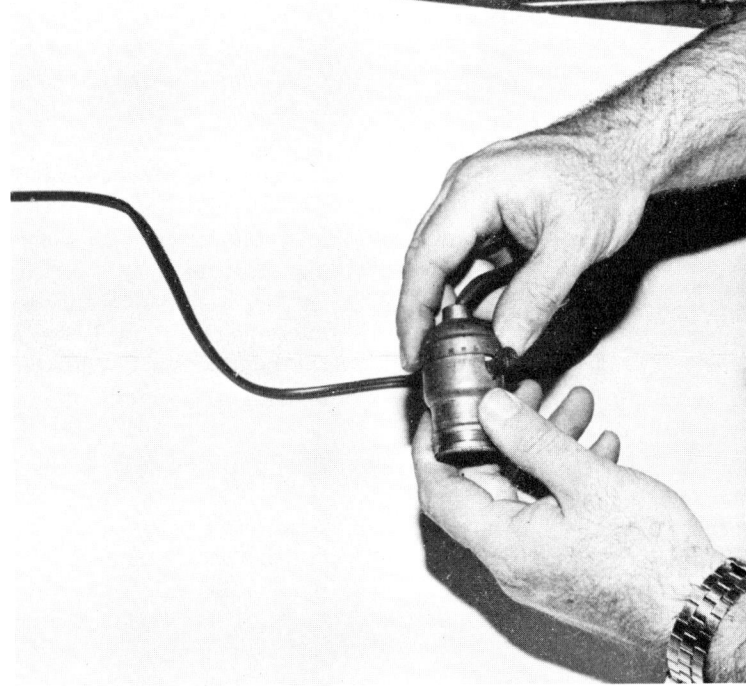

Electric Lamps 53

20
Hair Dryers

The hair dryer consists of a heating coil or element through which air is blown by an electric fan. The fan can have a controllable speed that is operated by a switch with more than one position. The various "speeds" can control fan speed, as is usually the case, although there are hair dryers that offer various heat levels by controlling the amount of voltage applied through the heating coil.

If the problem is an electrical one, you'll be able to diagnose it by what is — or isn't — happening. If the unit gets hot but does not blow out the air, the trouble might be in your fan (or the wiring to it). If the unit blows only cold air, the trouble most likely is in your heating unit. The only other possibility is that nothing at all happens — no air blows and it isn't hot!

The hand-held blower types of dryers can be opened easily by removing the screws that hold the two halves together. You might find a unit that also has a round spring at one end that fits into a groove near the end. This groove might be covered with a metallic vinyl tape that you will have to remove to get at the spring.

The cassette types may fool you at first. At least one of these must be opened by removing four screws at the bottom. These are actually located under a foam plastic pad which serves as a mar-proof base for the unit when it is rested on furniture. To get at the screws, you must peel the foam pad aside.

Once inside a visual inspection can be most revealing. Look for broken connections or shorts. If you are not getting any heat, put your ohmmeter across the heating unit. You should be able to read a very high resistance, but the heating unit should show this high-resistance continuity.

At least one manufacturer uses a vane switch in the air path so that unless the fan is blowing, the heat cannot come on. Make sure that if such a switch is used, it is not stuck in the "Off" position. In one other case, a manufacturer produces a "two-speed" model which uses a small solid-state rectifier. With the rectifier out of the circuit, the unit blows full blast. Switch to the next position, put the rectifier back in the circuit, and the unit operates at half speed and half heat. This rectifier is recognizable by its usually cylindrical shape and will have two wires coming out of it. If you suspect this unit remove it from the circuit and check it with your ohmmeter.

Checking these units is tricky. With the positive ohmmeter lead on one terminal of the rectifier you will read a very low resistance when you touch the negative lead to the other terminal. Reverse the leads and you will read a very high resistance. This device, called a diode, permits the flow of current in one direction and impedes the flow in the other direction. As alternating current flows half a cycle in one direction and another half cycle in the other, the diode (for that's what the rectifier is) will reveal high resistance one way, low resistance the other way. If you get any other kind of reading, get a new diode. You can obtain a suitable replacement at any local electronics shop.

If the fan isn't functioning and you're sure that it is getting proper voltage, try removing the plug (safety first) and rotating the fan blades with your fingers. If the fan is bound up, try lubricating the fan motor with ordinary household oil. If you can free the stuck blades, you might just restore the unit to operation.

Always take care when using light machine oil or household oil that you do not get any on plastic parts or wire insulation or, for that matter, on rubber parts or grommets. Oil will attack these surfaces and spoil them. If you do get some oil where it shouldn't be, wipe it up.

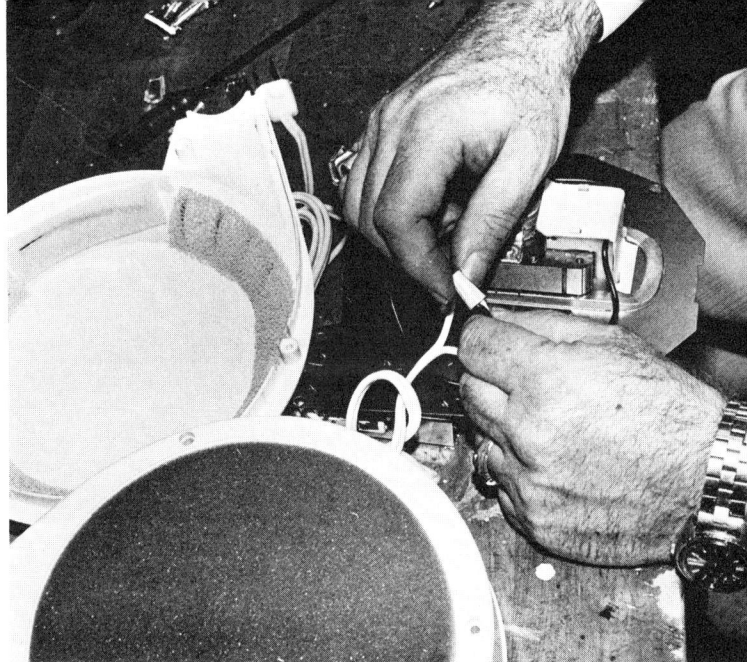

Replace the wire nut by twisting the wires and screwing the nut over them.

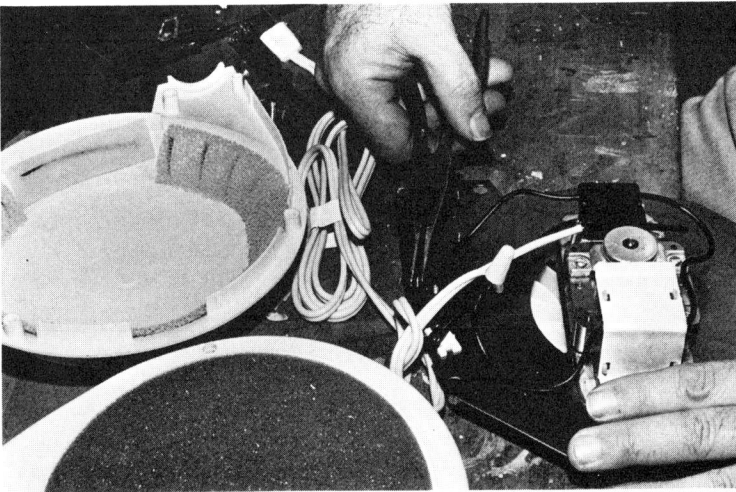

To remove the cover over the heating coil, rotate the four mounting tabs so they align with the slots.

The heating coil consists of a coiled length of heating element that is wound over a heat resistant form.

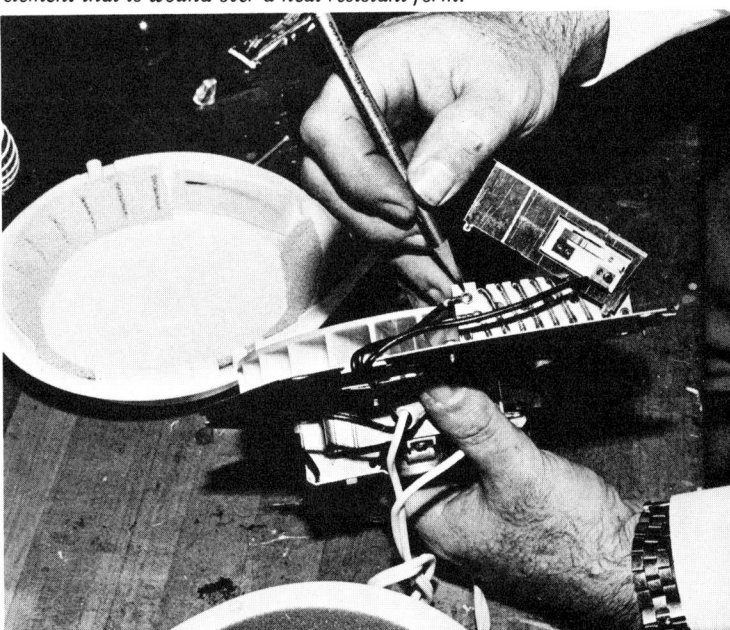

A threaded device known as a wire nut holds the three connecting wires of a hair dryer in place. To remove, simply rotate clockwise.

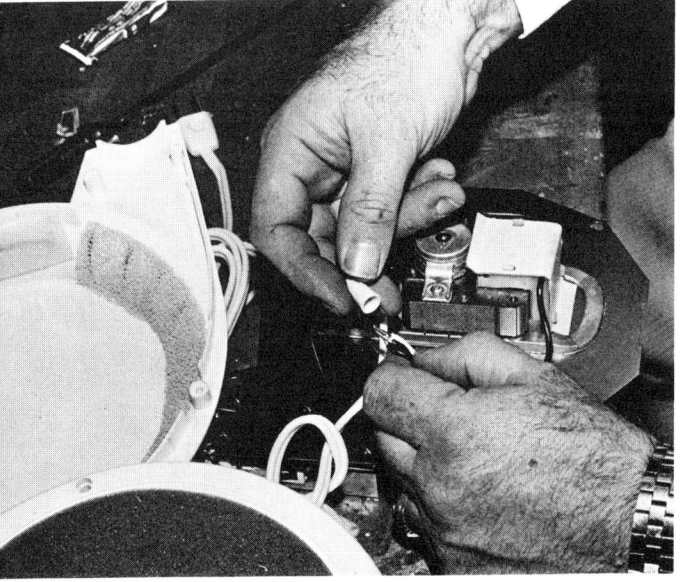

21
Electric Heaters

Because so little can go wrong with these units, diagnosis and repair are relatively simple.

In every type of unit the critical component is the wire coil which must be continuous from one end to the other. You can test this by placing your ohmmeter on the highest range, unplugging the unit from the wall outlet, and measuring the resistance across the terminal plugs. If the coil is continuous, you will get a high-resistance reading with the switch (if there is a switch on your unit) in the "On" position.

If your heater has a multi-position switch for different heat ranges, make this test with the switch in each position. You should get meter deflection in each range. If this does not happen, you must determine if you get deflection in any switch position. Deflection in one position of the switch and not in the others denotes a bad switch. No deflection indicates a bad coil.

Changing the coil is a relatively easy matter except for one caution that must be observed. You will note that the coil now in your heater is extended. The replacement coil is tightly wound. The old coil, having long been annealed by heating, will be brittle. The new coil will be relatively flexible.

Remove the old coil by disconnecting it from the terminal screws. Now attach one end only of the new coil. You have to stretch it slowly as you put it into place, so that it will extend and reach from the first terminal screw, through and around the insulators, to the other terminal screw. Your task is to stretch it in such a way as to evenly space the coils. If you have not stretched it quite enough, start over at the beginning and stretch it a bit more. Caution: don't overstretch the coils, for you won't be able to "shrink" them again and you have to use the full length of this resistance wire. You can't simply stretch it tightly and then clip away the excess. If you overstretch, you're going to have to start over with a new length of coil.

You might also have a bad switch. Believe it or not, the best source for exact replacement switches will be your local electronics supply shop. Remove the old switch by unsoldering the wires; make a small sketch of which wires go where. Remove the control knob from the shaft of the switch and you will see a half-inch hexagonal nut that you can unscrew from the threaded shank of the switch. This will allow the old switch to drop into your hand.

22
Electric Mixers

If the mixer fails, the problem will be an electrical one. The drive motor, of course, must be treated like any other motor so far as servicing is concerned. The speed controls are to be treated as any other sophisticated electronic circuitry is.

If the unit is an inexpensive one, the chances are that the motor is underrated for its job; it will object to the stress resulting from the pull of kneaded dough by stalling and/or burning out. However, many of these motors are protected by a fail-safe device called a thermal cutout. When the motor strains, it overheats, and the thermal cutout opens to break the circuit until the motor cools down again. When the motor *does* cool down, the thermal cutout restores itself automatically, and everything starts to work once more. The idea here is that if the unit does stop, always allow it to cool down and then try it once more — before you start opening things up to try and find what's wrong.

These units are not overly complex, but they do have an electric motor, a speed-controlling switch, and a geared coupling to the beater shafts. The first thing you have to do if you can't re-start the unit after a cool down period is to isolate the source of the problem. This is done by a process of elimination of possible faults.

Start by dropping out the beaters, remove the dress trim and covers from the motor head, and look for trouble in the form of open circuits or disconnected wiring. In checking the wires, tug gently at them to make sure that all are making good and proper contact. Be certain that no oxidation is present, and clean the contacts where you can. Your local electronics service supply shop will offer a liquid contact cleaner that you can swab over all contacts with a cotton swab.

If this still fails to restore proper operation, disconnect the electric motor from the control switch, and loosen the screws that hold the beater assembly to the shaft. With the motor thus freed of load on the one hand and control circuitry on the other, connect the motor terminals directly to a 115-volt source.

If the motor has clip-on contacts, you will find that it is relatively simple to solder a pair of leads with an AC plug to the back of these contacts in such a manner that when you unsolder them they will not interfere with remaking

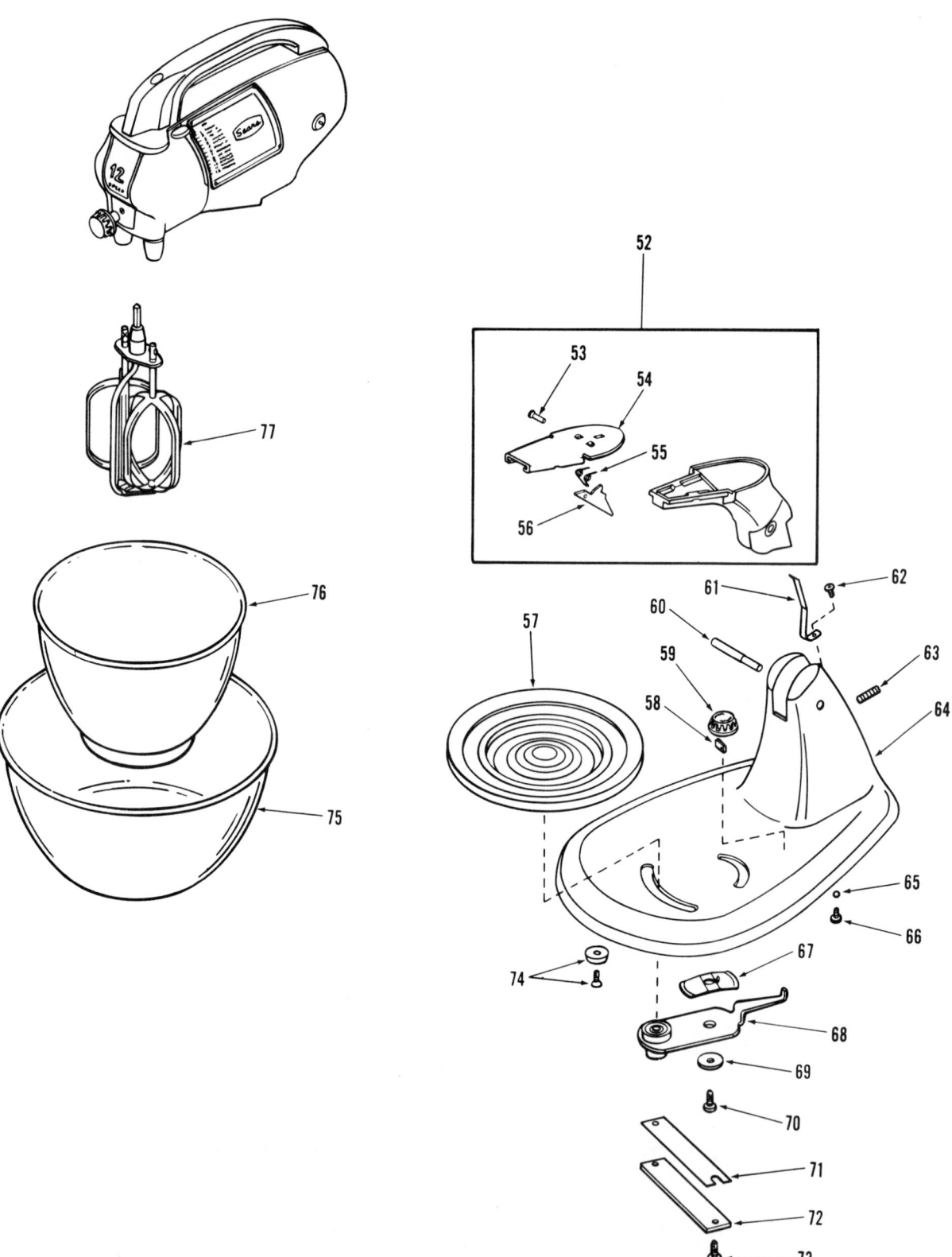

Parts illustrations for modern mixer.

Courtesy of Sears, Roebuck and Co.

REPAIR PARTS LIST

Key No.	Description
52	Motor Arm Complete
53	Retaining Pin
54	Saddle
55	Release Spring
56	Safety Catch
57	Turntable
58	Insert
59	Knob
60	Retaining Pin
61	Spring
62	*Screw #6-20 x 1/4 in. lg. Round Hd. Type B Self Tapping-Metal
63	Adjusting Screw
64	Base Complete
65	Binding Slug
66	Screw
67	Tension Spring
68	Lever Complete
69	*Washer 11/16 O.D. x .195 Hole x .064 Thk. Brass
70	*Screw #10-32 x 7/16 in. lg. Phillips Type 23 Thread Cutting
71	Bearing Strip
72	Support Strip
73	*Screw (2 Used) #10-16 x 1/2 in. lg. Phillips Type 25 Thread Cutting
74	Bumper & Screw (5 Used)
75	Large Bowl
76	Small Bowl
77	Beater Set

*Standard hardware item, may be purchased locally. *Courtesy of Sears, Roebuck and Co.*

the contacts later. Now connect the motor directly to your house current and see if it operates. If it does, then remove the test wiring you just installed. Your motor is all right and you must look elsewhere for your problem. If the motor does not operate, the problem is in the motor, and having isolated the problem, you can take corrective steps. (See the section on motor maintenance.)

If the motor is operating, locate the beater assembly, and try to operate this manually by turning the driven portion with your fingers. The chances are that it will either operate freely or not at all. This, however, is a straight mechanical device that is driven by the motor. If it is bound or seized, it will keep the entire unit from working. The problem may be a simple one, such as a need for lubrication, or it may be more complex, with the beater drive assembly having stripped, worn, or broken drive gears.

Lubrication is an easy matter. You apply some light machine oil which will penetrate the dried-out gearing and get it to moving again. Later on you can use a heavier white grease to lubricate and keep the parts lubricated. If the gears are worn, stripped, or broken, they will have to be replaced. The easiest solution will be to replace the entire geared assembly, if you can get such a replacement

Electric Mixers

from your dealer. If not, you may choose to simply replace the bad gears. Get replacements at your local authorized dealer and note how the gears are attached to the shafts. If they are held with set screws, there is no problem at all. Just loosen the old gears, put the new ones in place, reassemble the unit and align the new gears. If they are "shrunk-fit" in place, you may have to use a torch and some elbow grease to expand the old gear and then drive the new one into place. We strongly urge the use of a new gear assembly to correct this problem.

However, there is every possibility that the motor and the gear train are in fine order. Your problem might be in the electronic speed-controlling circuit, operated by the switch or knob at the top of the unit.

This is also removable and replaceable by a new one from the manufacturer. Order the entire unit from the service shop. Make a simple pencil drawing of the old one, showing what color wire is connected to which terminals, so you can replace the old with the new when you get it, and do so properly.

Before ordering this replacement, however, remove the old unit and open it up. These control devices are usually mounted in plastic blocks and are covered by a plastic sheet held by small sheet-metal screws with Phillips heads. Remove the screws and you'll find an assortment of components on the inside.

Look these over carefully, seeking out obvious damage. You might find a resistor that has burned open. Perhaps by replacing this burned out resistor, you can restore operation easily. The usual procedure in making such a replacement is to unsolder the old component and wire and solder the new one in its place. Sometimes, in doing this, you can create havoc with the other parts of the circuit, so we will instead show you how to replace a component the easy way:

Do not unsolder the old component. Instead, clip the old one out by using your wire cutter and clip close to the body of the resistor you are going to replace. Straighten what remains of the connecting wires and then form the leads of the new component into spirals by wrapping them tightly around a piece of wire of the same diameter as the remaining wires that were left when you clipped the old part out. Make the spirals about one-eighth of an inch long. Clip away the excess wire from the spirals.

Now slip the spirals over the lead wires you left, crimp them with your pliers, and then solder to secure them in place. You have now replaced the component without endangering other parts.

If the motor of your electric mixer won't operate, the problem might be in the starter capacitor. Remove this by unsoldering the old one and replace it.

Apply a drop of oil to the mixer motor's shaft bearing.

23
Telephone Answering Machines

The telephone answering machine is a complex unit. There are, however, certain faults in them that you can remedy fairly easily and with little or no technical knowledge. If you do not get the unit repaired by following these steps, you will have done no damage to it and the repairman will save time (and your money) by not having to perform these steps.

Certainly, if the unit fails while under warranty, by all means refer it to the service shop. If you break the seals by opening the unit, you will have voided the warranty and may have to pay for extensive repairs.

If people try to telephone you and all they get is a busy signal, while the tape seems to be all used and won't rewind, it means that the tape end has disconnected itself from the take-up spool. Carefully open the unit after disconnecting it from the supply voltage, remove the various telephone connections, and locate the supply reel. You will see the loose end of the tape wound around this. The tape is small; the same size as is used in most cassette machines. Locate the end and, with a small pair of tweezers, pull sufficient slack out so that you can work with it. Because this end *must* be kept in place on the take-up reel, you can solve the problem with a small drop of red Glyptal varnish. Put the ball in place on the take-up reel and apply a small drop of the varnish over the tape end so it will be cemented permanently to the reel. If you use too much of the varnish, you will find that it will drip down and cement the reel to the deck. Now slip the tape between the heads and the pressure pads.

Another rather common problem that occurs is that after a while the recordings are so muddy that they are all but unintelligible. To correct this, you need a device called a degausser or demagnetizer. This is a transformer housed in a special casing with an on-off switch and a plastic-coated probe. You plug the unit into an alternating current source and press the button while holding it well away from the answering unit. Now, holding down the button, bring the probe into direct contact with each of the heads, except for the erase head, which is usually a piece of alnico magnet. You do *not* want to demagnetize this! Perform this operation without releasing the power button. When you have finished, move the degausser far away from the heads before releasing the switch.

The next step is to completely clean the heads. Using your fingernail, pull

Lubrication is required wherever metal bears on metal.

back on the pressure pads and release the tape. This will give you access to the tape heads. Using alcohol (or a standard head-cleaning chemical) and a cotton swab, clean the heads thoroughly until no more tape oxides (the brown stuff) appears on the swab. Now release the pressure pads and replace the tape in the slots. If you find that the pressure pads have become compressed, you can replace those too. Buy a new set of pads at any electronics supply house, cut them to size, then remove the old pads by scraping them off their holders. Press the new pads into place, and you're all set again.

You may also find that, if you bought the unit some time ago, you're in trouble with the telephone company, which will insist that an approved telephone coupler be used. If your unit does not have this type of coupler built into it, contact the manufacturer, who can supply, at a nominal cost, an outboard coupler that you can plug in.

Carefully lift the pressure pads away from the record/playback head, and clean away residual oxides with a Q-tip dipped in plain alcohol.

62   Small Appliance Repair

24
Electric Irons

Several things can go wrong with an electric iron. The usual complaint is that the iron does not heat. First make sure that the line cord is delivering the proper amount of electricity to the iron. If it is not, repair or replace the cord.

Electric iron cords are usually insulated with asbestos. If the cord has burned open, try removing either the plug or the socket, clip the wire and restrip it, then reconnect the plug or socket on the cord. This sort of repair will probably cost you a couple of inches of cord length, but this is not usually a problem. If the socket is a molded one, just replace the cord.

To replace a cord plug or socket, begin by purchasing a new one at your local hardware supplier. Clip off the old socket, and put it aside for now. Your wire cutters will remove this handily. Remove all vestiges of burned or hardened wire.

Using a sharp razor knife, carefully cut through the insulation cover, which will probably be of a woven fabric. Cut through for about two inches. Remove the excess fabric and dispose of it. Under this covering, you will find white asbestos insulation wrapped around the two plastic- or rubber-covered conducting wires. Remove this asbestos insulation until it is level with the fabric covering. Using the razor knife, carefully cut away the rubber insulation so that a half inch of bare wire is exposed at each wire end. Twist the wire strands of each wire together so that you now have two ends of wire, each twisted.

Take your new plug or socket apart: if it's a socket, remove the screw(s) that hold the halves together; if it's a plug, remove the cardboard insulator. You will see two small screws for making the electrical connections. Loosen these screws and pass one of the wires through the neck of the socket (or plug) and connect one exposed, twisted wire to each screw. Pass the wires around the screws in a clockwise direction and tighten the screws. Replace the cardboard insulator for the plug, reassemble the socket, and the job is done.

If you prefer, your local hardware dealer can provide you with a complete new cord, fully assembled and ready to plug in and use.

If the problem is not in the cord, remove the screws that hold the insulated handle and lift off the handle. This will reveal the screws that hold the sole plate to the upper housing. Remove those screws and then the sole plate, which will expose the heating element and the thermostat. All of this is done, of course, with the plug disconnected and the cord removed.

Using your ohmmeter, check the heating element for continuity, though the chances are that if the heating element has burned open, you'll see this plainly enough.

If the heating element has burned open, it must be replaced. You can obtain a new element either from your appliance repair supplier, any hardware store, or a lumber yard.

The heating element for an electric iron is usually wound on a shaped mica form. If your new element is pre-wound on a mica form, remove the old one, connect the new one in its place, and mount it in the iron's sole plate.

If the new one is a length of nichrome wire, carefully remove the old wire from the mica form and replace it with the new wire. Be sure that you do not clip or shorten the overall length of wire, as this is a resistance wire and the full length is needed to provide a resistive path for the current going through it.

If the problem does not appear to be in the heating element, it could be in the thermostat, which is variable and temperature sensitive. Move the thermostat adjustment to make sure that the lever is properly connected to the thermostatic unit. Some thermostats have a remote probe, which consists of two dissimilar wires connected together. If these have separated, you will have to replace the entire thermostatic element. It's always a good idea to replace the entire thermostatic unit if a failure occurs in any part of the controlling system.

Electric steam irons can have additional problems, usually caused by the clogging of dried-out minerals in the water. Tap water does contain a heavy mineral content and, depending on where you live, the amounts can vary. You'll see these at once in the form of a white residue when you open up the iron. They clog the water passages and fill the holes through which the steam is supposed to escape.

Getting rid of these solids is not an easy job. You can scrape with probes and flake some of it off, but the best bet we've found is to strip everything off the sole plate and bring it to an electroplating firm, where it can be acid-dipped.

Your best bet is to avoid the problem. Either use distilled water in your steam iron or buy one of the charcoal filter devices designed for this. You place the plastic filter into the water inlet on the iron and pour your tap water through the top of the filter. What goes into the iron is "purified" but not really distilled. It's better than having to take the iron apart every few months to get rid of the solids.

After disassembling the sole plate from the iron, you'll notice that the heating element is held by riveted washers. Heating element consists of copper tube filled with dry sand and having hot wire running through it.

Connections to and from the element can be remade with a soldering gun.

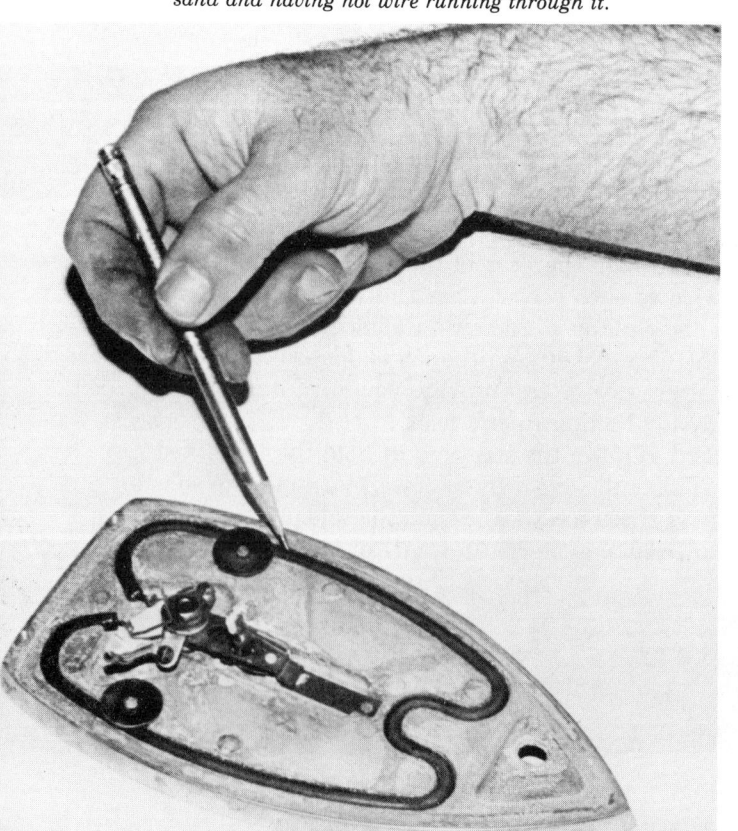

25
Electric Fans

The chances are that if your electric fan isn't operating, the first thing you have to do is clean it up. Fans move air at remarkable rates. As the blades travel at high speeds through the still air, they generate a static charge which seems to be just sufficient to attract globules of grease and bits of airborne dust, dirt, and lint.

We've found that the best way to do a clean-up is to begin by removing the blade guard from the fan. You'll see that this is held to the fan motor housing by three or four screws. Flat washers and lockwashers may also be used. We usually place such small hardware items in a glass dessert dish and fill the dish with a good-quality household degreaser so that these parts can be cleaned while we're working on the rest of the assembly. In fact, you can make a small basket by pressing a piece of screening to conform to the shape of the dessert dish so that parts retrieval is simplified. Lift out the basket and the parts can be allowed to drain.

With the guard removed, you'll locate a small collar that attaches the blades to the armature of the motor. This will be held in position by small set screws of either the Allen variety or the slotted type. Remove these screws and place them in the degreaser too. Now the blades assembly should slip off relatively easily. Take off the blades and proceed to clean them by using a cloth soaked in the degreasing fluid. Get the blades spotlessly clean; then, with the goo removed, you can immerse the blades in a solution of warm water and detergent and allow them to soak clean.

The motor housing may have a rear arm that protrudes from the back of the housing and couples to a fixed position on the fan's base. This arm is used to provide oscillation to the fan so that it will sweep an area instead of remaining in a fixed position. Usually a wing nut or a knurled thumbscrew is used to lock the arm and prevent oscillation. Or the fastener can be loosened so the arm oscillates the fan. Disassemble these parts and place them in the degreasing bath. Remove the motor housing from the motor, placing the motor assembly itself on a piece of newspaper. Put the housing components into the degreaser to clean. With the motor now out of the housing, try to rotate the armature shaft with your fingers. It should operate freely and smoothly. If it does not, look for obstructions. Check the condition of the brushes by opening the two

Removing the blade guard.

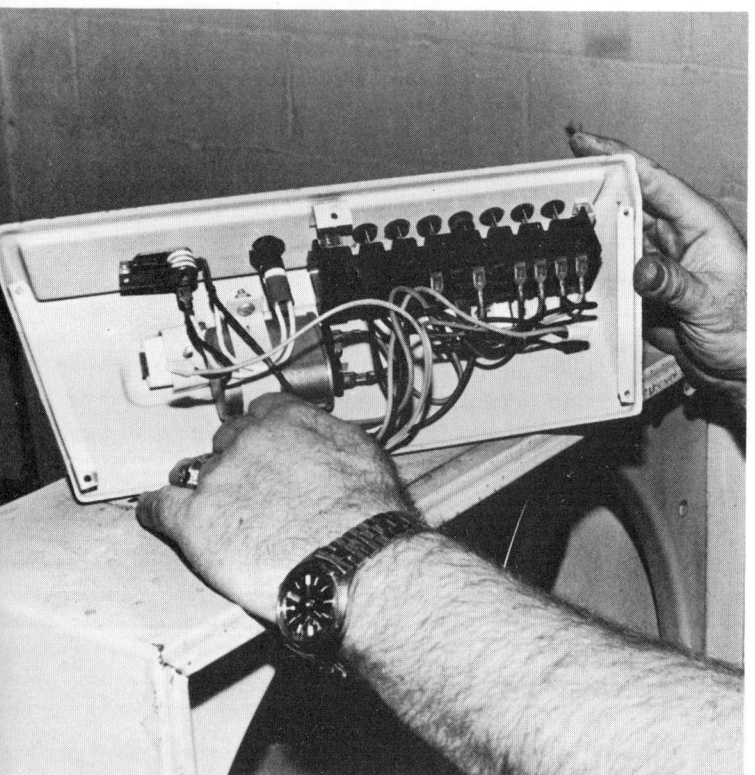
Upper control circuit

plastic or knurled caps. Be careful that the springs do not fly off. If the carbon brushes appear to be badly worn, obtain a new set and replace them. Clean the commutator segments also. Remove all traces of oxidation and see that the insulated spaces between the commutators are not bridged.

At this point, you should be able to reassemble the motor by reversing the disassembly procedure. As you do this, however, take care to rinse the degreaser agent completely from all parts, swish all parts in water to ensure that they are clean, and then immerse them in an alcohol bath which will remove all traces of water.

Wherever parts bear against one another, add proper lubrication. The bearings that support the ends of the armature shafts should be given a light coat of white grease. Where bare metal is exposed, it should be lightly sprayed with an aerosol machine oil which will prevent rust. And where metal bears on metal, such as in the oscillating control, you should apply a bit of light white grease or machine oil.

Be sure that you also examine the electrical wiring. You may find that the insulation has become hard and embrittled. Changing the wiring completely is not a difficult task, but it can make the difference between success and failure. Many of these fans are equipped with small rotary switches. It would not hurt to clean the contacts by spraying the switch with De-Oxid or a similar cleaning material. You can get this at any electronics supply shop.

You should be aware that oscillating fans can be locked so they do not oscillate by tightening down a thumbscrew on the oscillating mechanism. If your fan does not oscillate, check to see that this screw is loose.

In recent years large window fans have become very popular. These consist of a metal frame which is placed in the window opening, and the window is brought down on the top of the frame to lock it into position.

Supporting brackets from the edges of the frame to the center hold the motor, which supports the fan blades. Some of these window fans contain thermostats which turn the fan off when a preset temperature has been reached.

Other types employ a push button or rotary

switch arrangement which controls whether the fan will intake or exhaust air and will also set the speed of the fan.

If the fan has an electronic circuit to control the speed, you may find that the circuit is referenced to AC ground. This means that the ground return path of electricity may be directly tied to one of the legs of the AC plug. Usually, one side of the line in your home is at ground potential anyway, so with the plug in the wall socket, everything is as it should be, and the fan works just fine. However, that other lead carries 110 volts. If you insert the plug the wrong way, or if the isolation capacitor just happens to be shorted, you can get quite a jolt.

To avoid this, begin by placing your ohmmeter on one of the plug prongs and the other ohmmeter wire on a spot of bare metal on the fan's casing. If you get continuity, you've got a problem. Open up the fan by removing the case so that you can locate the isolation capacitor. You'll recognize it as the one connected to ground directly (to the metal frame). Replace this unit as quickly as possible.

If you want to use the fan anyway, there's a safe way to do this. Get a bottle of nail polish and mark the insulation on the side of the plug that is *not* connected to the frame of the fan. Then place your volt-ohm-milliameter on the AC volts scale, insert one lead into the nearest wall socket, and touch the other lead to the metal screw that holds the plate over the socket. (This is ground potential too.) If you do not get any reading, you're at the ground side. If you do, you're on the "hot" side, and can mark that side with nail polish as well. From now on, just plug the fan in so that the nail polish spot on the plug is nearest the nail polish spot on the outlet, and you'll have ground connected to ground so you don't electrocute yourself and make things hot when you're trying to cool off.

26
Cassette Players and Recorders

The cassette recorder has two problem areas. It is electro-mechanical, which means that while part of the assembly is electronic and requires only an occasional change of batteries, the mechanical parts can sometimes respond to a few carefully planned ministrations.

Inside the player/recorder you'll find a series of belts and you may find that one of the belts has slipped off its pulleys or idler wheels. The latter are used to retain belt tension. If the belt has slipped, you'll see where it belongs because you'll find undue slack in the belt and an idler wheel or pulley with no belt around it. Replace the belt so that proper tension seems to be restored, then increase the tension by locating one of the idlers that has a screw-loosening adjustable bracket. If the belt is broken, replace it with a direct-replacement type, available at any good electronics supply shop.

If you find that you can record and play on one tape and not on another, check the back edge of the cassette cartridge to see if the little square tabs may have broken off. These are used to depress a cut-off switch inside the machine and if you want to permanently preserve a tape, you snap off the tabs. This will keep the machine from recording. If the tab has inadvertently broken off, discard the tape and try another.

Sticky action in the cassette machine can be caused by the buildup of dirt and oxides on the various transport rollers and capstan. Use a cotton swab, some alcohol, and clean up everything. There are also various excellent tape cleaners.

If the mechanism itself seems to be sticking, apply some light machine oil (we prefer special lubricants made for this purpose) wherever metal bears on metal. Make sure you don't get oil on rubber or plastic parts, however, as this will wreak havoc on them and destroy or distort the rubber.

If the unit will play back a prerecorded tape but does not record on a new tape, the problem might be that the microphone is at fault and replacing the mike could restore the unit to operation. Certainly, other things can go wrong, but in this instance, the mike should be checked by plugging in another mike that is known to work. If you do not have a replacement mike at hand, you can still make an adequate test by unscrewing the black plastic shell over the mike plug, and then touching the center conductor with your finger while the unit is on "Record." There is no danger in this, as no voltage is present at this terminal. Hold your finger on the contact for a moment or two and then rewind and play back. If you hear a loud hum, it indicates that the machine is good. Have the mike tested.

You may have everything working, but there's a loud rattling noise coming out of the speaker along with the music or talk. This could indicate that there's a bit of grit or dirt lying on the speaker cone or that the speaker cone is torn.

If the cone is not too badly damaged, but just has a rip or tear in it, you can usually repair this yourself. Obtain some speaker-cone cement from your local electronics shop. With the "works" removed from the cabinet paint a broad swath of the cement along the tear on the top and bottom of the speaker. Get some ordinary toilet tissue and cut ribbons of the tissue at least as wide and as long as the tear. Soak the strips with the cement and place the wet strips over the tear on both sides of the speaker, building up layer upon layer until the tear is mended. The speaker may sacrifice some quality, but should perform again without the rattling.

People will drop a recorder/player occasionally and crack the case. You can generally effect a satisfactory repair of the case using epoxy cement and some imagination, but be certain that the case is all that's broken.

Threading the drive belt through grooved pulleys.

Soldering a connection.

Cassette Players and Recorders

27
Electric Knife Sharpeners

The usual knife sharpener will consist of a carborundum stone that is shaped and beveled to put a proper edge on a knife blade. There are two common problems that can affect such sharpeners. When a blade is inserted and the motor is turned on, the carborundum stone will rotate and by drawing the knife blade through the stone's bevel, you hone the blade. The stones have been known to shatter. Should this happen, no repair at all can be made short of replacing the stone.

You may also find that the motor operates but the stone does not rotate, which indicates that the driving belt has either broken or slipped its pulley. In the latter case, it's a relatively simple matter to remove the housing and replace the belt. If the belt has broken, a new belt must be installed.

Removing the plastic housing is the first problem you will encounter. We have come across two distinct types of methods used to hold the plastic housings in place. You may find two or three recessed screws that are accessible from the back. Removing these screws will cause the housing to yield and the back to come off, leaving the front of the unit with all the components attached there. In the other type of sharpener, the recessed metal base fits into four plastic lugs at the bottom of the housing. Gently pry these away from the metal base with a large-blade screwdriver, slipping the base past the lugs until all four lugs have been moved past the metal base, at which time the base can be removed from the plastic housing.

There is the danger that the lugs will snap off. This has happened on more than one occasion, but do not worry about this. Because the plastic lugs are under the unit, they will not show, and you can easily cement a lug back into place using one of the new polymeric cements which will hold tightly and restore the unit.

Should the plastic casing itself develop a crack or fissure, the best way to correct this is again with one of the polymer-type cements. Fasten a heavy rubber band around the unit to close up the fissure, then apply a bit of the cement along the crack. Capillary action will draw the cement the full length of the crack and quickly effect a repair.

Should you find that the belt has slipped its pulley, replace the belt in the pulley groove. Then, by applying finger pressure, check its tautness. The belt might have stretched and become too loose, in which case a new belt is needed.

Because these belts are also used as speed reducers, running from a small drive pulley to a larger driven pulley, some whipping can take place. You can obtain a belt dressing compound at any hardware store to apply to the belt. It will inhibit slippage and provide better traction for the belt in the pulley groove.

While you've got the unit apart, apply a drop or two of oil to the moving metal parts, keeping the oil from rubber components.

Many people make the mistake of applying too much pressure to the knife blade while drawing it through the sharpener. This results in severe strain on the motor and shortens the expected life of the unit. Only the slightest pressure is required.

You must remember that an electric knife sharpener is basically an electric motor that operates the metal blades through a geared mechanism. Mass production economies and low-cost modern plastics sometimes result in gears that are constructed of nylon or even less costly materials. When the gears do fail, generally several of the gear cogs or teeth will be stripped from the gear. This will be evidenced by the fact that the motor runs, but the blades do not operate. To verify this, you have to take the knife apart and carefully examine the gears. Sometimes the gear can part with some teeth and still operate, albeit inconsistently. It depends on how many teeth left the gear, and where the missing teeth are located.

You have to replace such a gear, for it cannot be repaired.

The gears are usually held in place either by a shrink fit or by a spline or clip arrangement.

If it is a shrink fit, the easiest way to remove the old gear is with a gear puller. If you do not have one, a battery-cable puller from your local auto supply store will do. Pressing the new gear on will require that you dismount the geared shaft so you can apply proper pressure. To help in this, we like to place the gear in boiling water and the shaft in the refrigerator. This enables the gear to enlarge and the shaft to shrink so that the assembly is much easier.

The spline arrangement uses a small wedge that fits into a groove on the shaft and mates with a groove in the gear. First align the two grooves, then press the spline into place.

The clip set-up uses a small C-washer that snaps over the gear and into a groove around the shaft. Make certain that you do not lose the washer, for these have a tendency to snap off once they are released and lose themselves in the carpet! To replace the washer, first make sure that the gear is properly seated on the shaft to expose the groove. Then hold the washer in alignment with a needle-nose pliers or small tweezers, and press it home.

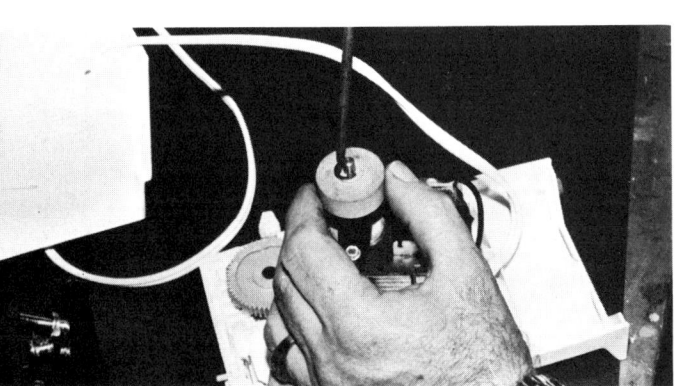

To remove the carborundum wheel first pry away the C-washer with a screwdriver.

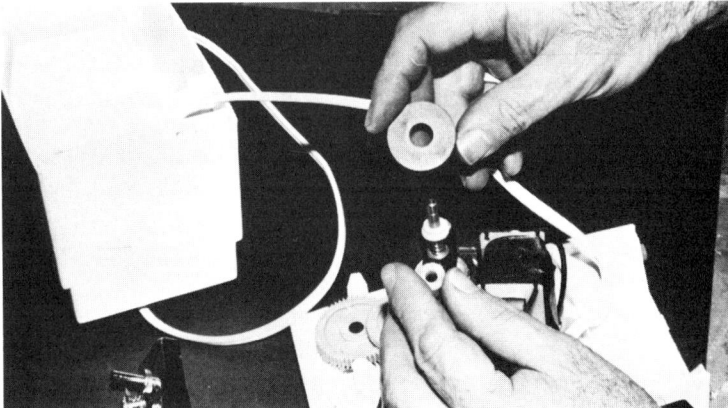

With the C-Washer removed, you can lift off the old stone and replace it.

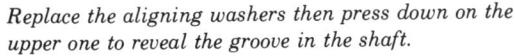

Replace the aligning washers then press down on the upper one to reveal the groove in the shaft.

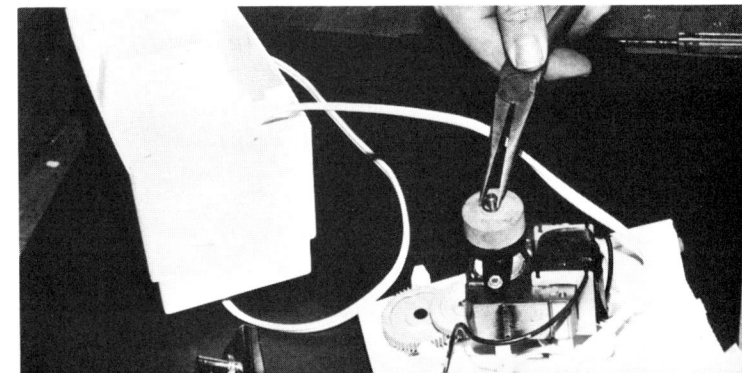

28
Electric Can Openers

The electric can opener is such a simple device that the things that can go wrong with it are easily repaired. The only real problem is parts accessibility, and again, due to the simplicity of this appliance, parts can often be substituted with no harm done or loss in operating efficiency.

If the motor operates properly but the can will not rotate under the cutting blade, then the drive belt has broken. You know the motor is operating, because you can hear it and feel it. To correct this problem you must get inside the housing. You will find four screws at the bottom holding a metal base plate to the plastic housing. Remove the screws and the housing should slip off easily. On less expensive units four plastic lugs, molded to the housing, must be carefully pried apart so the base plate can slip out and away.

If the belt has actually broken, the answer is a replacement belt. To replace the belt, measure the diameter of the drive wheel and the diameter of the driven pulley. Multiply the diameter of each wheel by *pi* (3.14), which will give you the circumference. Divide the result by two and note the result, adding the two results together. Now measure the actual distance from the outside edge of the drive wheel to the outside edge of the driven pulley, multiply by two, and add this to the previous result, which will give you the circumference of the new belt you need. It's always a good idea, when you're buying a replacement belt, to get one a bit smaller to compensate for stretch.

Where do you buy a new belt? The best source we've found is your local electronics supply shop, where they have assorted-size belts for use in phonographs or tape recorders. You can usually pick up a whole assortment for a modest price.

To install the new belt, place it over the drive wheel (the bigger one) and then stretch it so that it slips into the groove of the driven pulley. You should take advantage of the fact that the unit is open to apply a bit of oil to the moving parts, but not to the new belt.

You might want to sharpen or hone the cutting wheel, too. We've found that the easiest way to do this is to remove the cutting wheel by taking out the screw that holds it. Place a longer screw of the same size through the wheel, add a lockwasher and a nut, and snub these down good and tight. Place the remaining shank of the screw into the chuck of your high-speed drill and when the drill is turned on, the cutting wheel will spin madly. Hold a carborundum stone against the cutting edge at the same angle as the wheel's bevel and you'll soon have the wheel better than new.

Some can openers do not use drive belts, but employ a nylon-geared arrangement for positive and silent drive. Examine the gears carefully; if one is stripped of its cogs, you will have to replace the gear. Your local authorized service dealer might be willing to sell you a replacement for you to install yourself. If not, take the remains of the old gear, along with the mating gear, to an industrial supply dealer (see your "Yellow Pages") and the chances are that they will be able to provide an exact replacement for you.

If a can opener is dropped the case may crack. Since some of the less-expensive units are built into the cases, using the case as a support member, such damage will render the unit useless until it is repaired. Begin by removing all the parts from the case and then fit the case pieces together to ascertain that you have all the parts. Having done so, use either a good epoxy cement or one of the new polymeric adhesives to reassemble the case. You can use rubber bands or self-adhesive tape to hold the parts together while they set. After the cement has completely dried, sand the outer surfaces to even the cement bonds and to roughen the surface. Spray the surface with a good-quality enamel in a spray can and allow it to dry thoroughly before touching it. Reassemble the components into the case, and there you are.

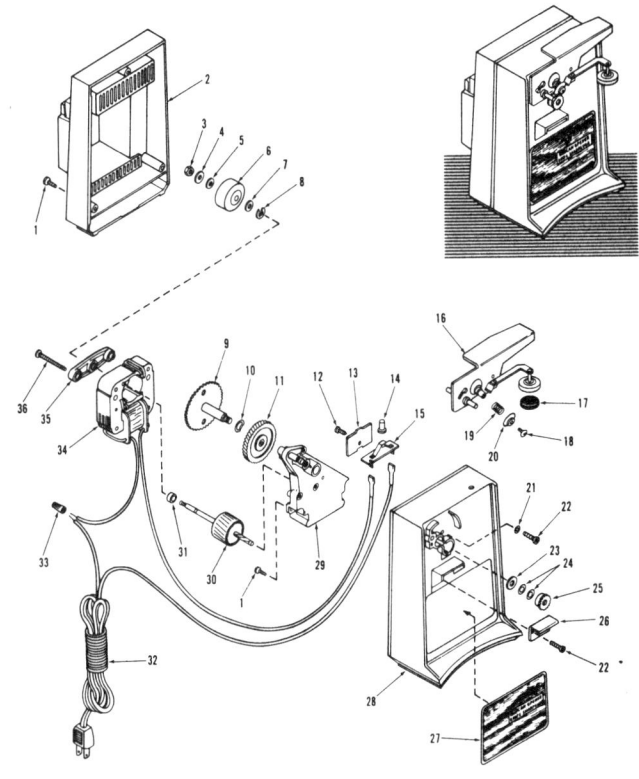

Key No.	Description
1	*Screw (5 Used) #8-18 x ½ in. Phillips Type 25
2	Rear Housing
2	Rear Housing
2	Rear Housing
3	*Nut—Special
4	*Washer 9/16 in. O.D. x 13/64 Hole x .032 Thick Steel
5	*Washer 7/16 in. O.D. x .220 Hole x .031 Thick Fibre
6	Grinding Wheel
7	*Washer 7/16 in. O.D. x .200 Hole x .031 Thick Fibre
8	Retaining Ring
9	Master Gear
10	Spring Washer
11	Idler Gear
12	*Screw #6 x 3/8 inch Phillips Type B Sheet Metal
13	Switch Cover
14	Switch Button
15	Switch Assembly
16	Lever Handle Complete
17	Magnet
18	*Screw #8-32 x ¼ in. Phillips Truss Head
19	Spring
20	Cutter Wheel
21	*Washer 3/8 in. O.D. x .156 Hole x .020 Thick Steel
22	*Screw (3 Used) Special HI-LO
23	*Washer 13/32 in. O.D. x .265 Hole x .025 Thick Steel
24	*Washer (AS REQ.) .370 in. O.D. x .265 Hole x .008 Thick Steel
25	Drive Wheel
26	Bottle Opener
27	Nameplate
28	Front Housing
28	Front Housing
28	Front Housing
29	Motor Frame Assembly
30	Rotor Assembly
31	Spacer
32	Cord Assembly
33	Wire Nut
34	Stator Complete
35	Bearing Housing
36	*Screw (2 Used) #6-20 x 1 11/16 in. Phillips Type 25

*Standard hardware item, may be purchased locally.

Courtesy of Sears, Roebuck and Co.

Parts illustrations for can opener/knife sharpener.

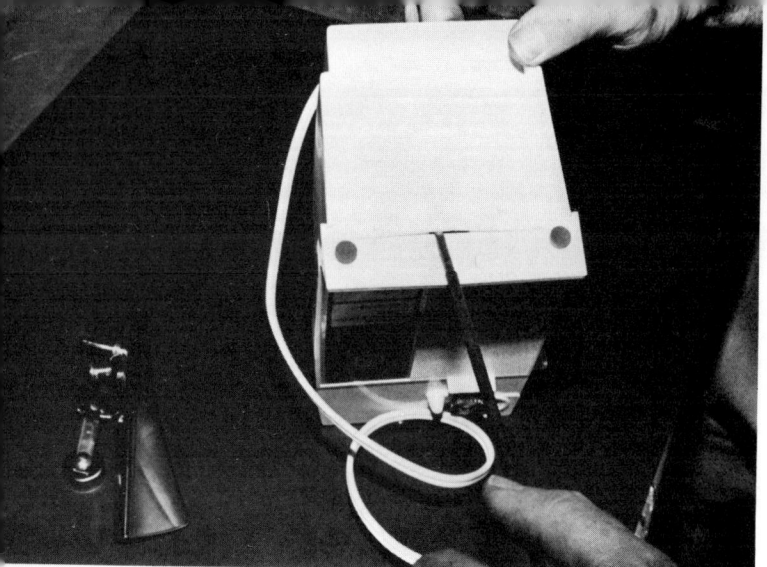

Pry up the rear apron with a sharp screwdriver to disassemble.

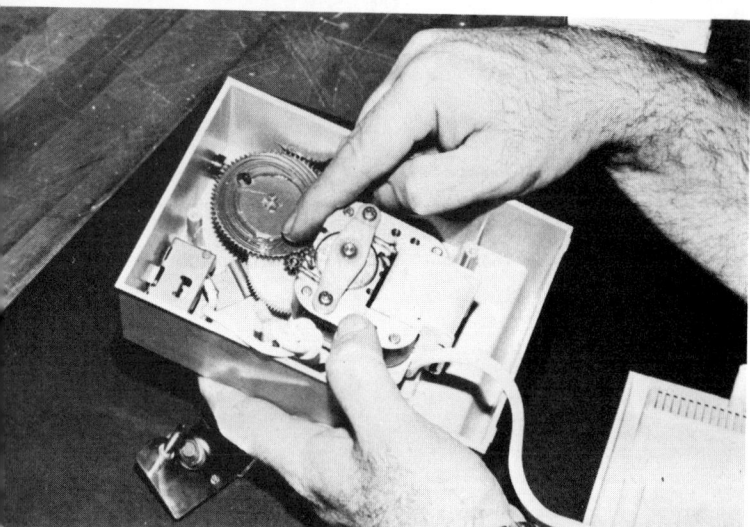

Apply a heavy film of grease to the drive wheel.

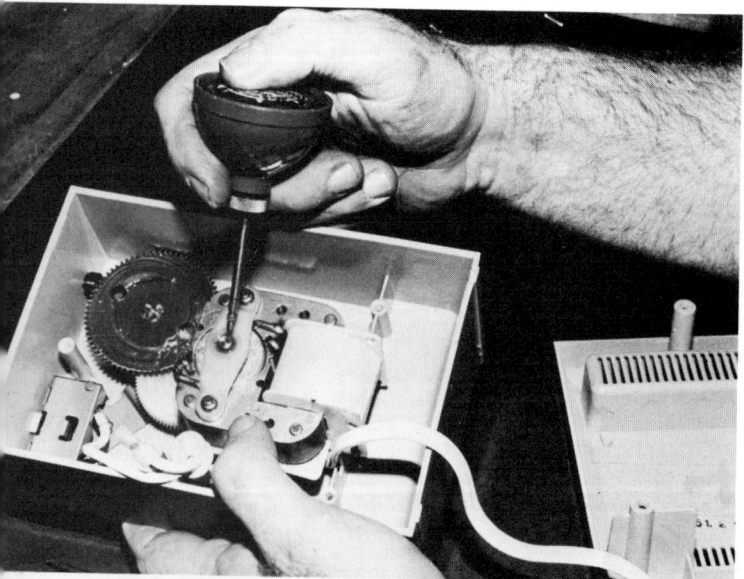

To keep the motor running with the least resistance, apply a drop of light machine oil to the exposed motor shaft bearing.

29
Malted Milk Machines

The malted milk machine is one of the simplest electric appliances you can service. It consists of a stand, at the top of which is mounted an electric motor. The motor shaft is coupled to a beater unit and the operation is controlled by a concealed switch that is actuated when the mixing cup is put in place on the machine. Being so basic, the malted milk machine is practically self-analyzing!

One of the first indicators of trouble will be the motor housing overheating. This means that the motor is straining and not venting properly. To avoid major repairs, this is the time to take corrective steps.

Unplug the unit and remove the motor housing to expose the motor. Make sure that the housing is completely clean inside and out and that all vent holes are free of dirt and dust. Because the brushes tend to spark at the commutators, an electrostatic charge can build and this will attract and hold dirt and grease. The vent holes fill quickly so that the motor doesn't "breathe" properly. It will soon overheat, leading to even more trouble.

While you've got the unit apart, check the brushes and check to see that sufficient lubrication is in place. A close look at the motor will reveal one of two things: you'll find small, spring-loaded caps over the grease cups or small holes marked "oil." In either case, apply some lube in the form of white grease in the grease cups or motor oil in the holes.

Another common problem is switch failure. Examine the switch carefully to see if a replacement is necessary. The switch is an ordinary, easy-to-obtain unit that is fitted with various types of actuator arms. Now an exact replacement from the manufacturer will consist of the switch *and* actuators (which will cost a good deal). However, your local electrical supply shop will usually yield an exact replacement switch mechanism at a small price. All you have to do is remove the old actuating mechanism and attach it to the new switch.

We have also seen some cases in which the beater shaft has become disconnected from the motor's armature. Remember that a lot of vibration does occur and the screws that hold the shafts together can work loose. Reattaching this is fairly simple. You put the shaft coupling back in place and tighten the small Allen screws with an Allen wrench.

Sure. Except that you haven't taken any steps to see that it doesn't happen again! Whenever a screw that is meant to hold forever works loose, we like to apply a bit of Scru-Lok or similar adhesive that works into the threads and keeps the screw from getting loose again. You can get this adhesive at any well-equipped hardware store.

The beater blades of a malted milk machine are formed of two washers with wavy edges. These are held to the shaft by a screw and a pair of mating bushings. Should these vibrate loose, restore them to position, using a bit of the thread sealer, and tighten it up.

FAULT-ANALYSIS CHART

APPLIANCE	SYMPTOM	SUGGESTED STEPS
Electric Toaster	Does not heat	Check element continuity Check line cord.
	Does not pop up	Clean crumb tray and apply lube to mechanism.
	Burns toast	Check thermostat; replace if necessary
Toaster Oven	Does not heat	Check continuity of heating elements. Replace those burned open.
	Door does not open	See that operating parts are not clogged; apply small amount of lube.
	Operates on high only	Check control wiring for short circuit. Replace, if necessary.
Electric Clock	Noisy, does not keep accurate time	Invert entire clock and allow to run upside down for about a week.
	Does not operate at all	Check wiring for open circuit. Replace clock motor.
Electric Carving Knife	Does not operate	Check wiring; remove blades; see that motor functions.
	Operates but is noisy	Remove blades and check to see that sufficient lube is in place. Check the nylon worm gear.
Meat Slicer	Blade does not rotate	Reread chapter on motor operated devices; check brushes.
	Blade does not cut	Could need sharpening. Use carborundum stone.
	Motor does not turn blade at proper speed	Disassemble unit and completely clean and degrease.

Small Appliance Repair

Vibrator	Does not operate	Check motor and wiring.
	Motor runs but unit does not vibrate	Check eccentric to see that it is properly attached.
Vacuum Cleaner	Motor does not work	Check switch first; if all right, check motor.
	Motor works, but no vacuuming	Check that all hoses are clear, free of dirt, and that new bag is installed.
	Unit overheats, stops	Indicates need for lubrication on all metal-bearing surfaces.
Blender	Does not operate	Remove bowl and check to see if motor works. Jump wire past control to motor to isolate problem.
	Wrong speeds or problem with controls	Replace control element. Check for loose wiring.
Electric Shaver	Does not operate	Remove shaver head and see if motor works. If so, check to see that shaver head is free.
	Motor operates but does not cut	If blade action is free sharpen or hone blades. Apply light oil to moving parts.
Air Freshener Humidifier	Motor does not work	Check setting of control.
	Belt does not move	Check belt tautness, tighten and restaple if required.
	Does not operate	Check water level and float switch.
Electric Blanket	Control does not function	Check that thermostat is not stuck or bound.
	Operates sporadically	Remove plug-in control from blanket; clean away any oxidation.
Electric Pencil Sharpener	Motor does not work	Check wiring. Check pressure switch.
	Motor works but does not cut pencils	Check blade fastener.
	Cuts on one side only	Blade out of alignment.

Fault-Analysis Chart

Phonograph/Stereo	No operation at all	Check fuse(s).
	Turntable rotates but no sound	Amplifier or speaker. See that both are connected.
	Speaker hums but turntable does not rotate	Check drive idler. Lube metal moving parts.
	Does not change records or record change cycle slow	Too many records on spindle. Remove to lighten weight.
	Only one channel functions	Check setting of balance control; see that mode switch is on "stereo."
Electric Lamp	Does not light	Check wiring. Replace lamp.
	3-way lamp works only on one or two positions	Replace lamp or unplug and raise socket contacts.
	Switch is loose or does not function	Rewire lamp and replace socket.
	Cord frayed or worn	Replace cord and plug.
Hair Dryer	Blows cold air only	Heating element faulty.
	Heats up but does not blow	Fan problem. Check to see if motor is functioning. If it does, check coupling to fan blade.
	Operates at single speed only	Switch control at fault. Replace.
Electric Heater	Does not operate at all	Check wiring, thermostat control, and on-off switch.
	Will not turn off	Check setting of thermostat. Replace faulty thermostat if necessary.
Electric Mixer	Motor does not operate	Check motor by bypassing control circuitry. If the motor functions, the problem is in controls.
	Control problem	Replace entire control unit.
	Bowl does not rotate	Disassemble, clean, and lubricate lazy Susan.
Telephone Answering Machine	Sound low or garbled	Clean and demagnetize tape heads.
	Answer message not working	Answer tape broken. Open machine and splice.
	All tape on take-up spool	Tape detached from supply spool. Re-fix.

	Tape bunches up	Check felt pads on drum brakes.
	Does not erase on rewind	Erase magnet not operating. Replace.
Electric Iron	Does not heat	Check line cord, and thermostat control.
	Does not generate steam	Check inside of steam outlet holes.
	Heats to maximum heat only	Thermostatic control not functioning or stuck. Replace.
Electric Fan	Does not operate	Check switch and motor.
	Does not oscillate	Clean and lubricate moving components.
	Loud "clicking" sound	Fan blades hitting guard. Bend guard to fix.
Cassette Player/ Recorder	Tape moves but no sound	Insert prerecorded tape, see if unit plays back. If not, problem is in playback function.
	Problem in playback	Turn volume full up, use new battery, touch contact of playback head and listen for hum.
	No hum	Replace playback amp.
	No record function	Try recording a tape and playback on another machine.
	Does not record	Replace record head. If no improvement, replace record electronics.
	Tape does not move	Try different tape. Check to see that motor is operating, and all belts are in proper position.
	Garbled sound	Clean and demagnetize tape heads.
	Flutter or "wow"	Clean all capstans and idlers.
Electric Knife Sharpener	Motor does not work	Check motor; replace if sealed unit type.
	Motor works but sharpening blades do not rotate	Check belt and replace if required. Lubricate as needed.
Electric Can Opener	Motor does not operate	Check wiring and switch. Check motor.
	Motor operates but can does not move.	Check and replace belt or drive components.

Fault-Analysis Chart 79

Malted Milk Machine	Does not operate	Check motor by bypassing switch. If motor is okay, replace switch.
	Motor operates but beater does not turn	Beater-to-motor shaft coupling is loose. Tighten.
	Motor housing very hot	Open casing, clean all air vents, and apply oil to shaft and bearings. Check brushes.

Index

Blenders
  blade sharpening, 35
  electronic switches in, 36–38

Can openers
  belt replacements, 72
  gear replacements, 73
  sharpening, 72–73

Carving knives, electric
  battery operated, 27
  part replacements for, 26–27
  sharpening, 26

Cassette players/recorders
  cleaning, 68
  defective speakers, 69
  mechanical malfunctions, 68
  microphones, 68–69

Clocks
  fit-ups for, 23, 24
  gearing mechanisms, 24
  motors, 23

Electric blankets
  control units, 45–46

Electric heaters
  coil replacements, 56
  defective switches, 56

Electric shavers
  cleaning, 41–42
  sharpening, 40, 42

Fans
  defective switches, 66–67
  grounds, 67
  motors, 65–66

Fault analysis chart, 76–80

Hair dryers
  defective switches, 54–55
  fan malfunctions, 55

Humidifiers
  defective belts, 43
  defective switches, 43

Irons
  cord replacement, 63–64
  cleaning, 64
  heating elements and thermostats, 64

Knife sharpeners
  belt replacements, 70–71
  stripped gears, 71

Lamps
  defective sockets, 51–52

Malted milk machines
  overheating, 75
  switch replacement, 75

Meat slicers
  cleaning, 29
  sharpening, 28
  switch replacement, 29

Mixers
  beater drive assemblies, 59
  motors in, 57–59
  switches, 60

Motors
  cleaning of, 17
  general principles of, 16–17
  rebuilding of, 17, 32–33
  synchronous, 23

Pencil sharpeners
  defective switches, 47–48
  lamp replacement, 48
  sharpening, 48

Phonographs
  defective turntables, 49–50
  loose wires, 49

Safety precautions, 8–10
Soldering, 9, 12–13

Telephone answering machines
  demagnetizing & cleaning heads, 61–62
  reconnecting tapes, 61

Thermal cutouts, 17, 35, 57

Toasters
  cleaning, 19–20
  heating elements, 19

Toaster ovens
  infrared rod replacement, 21
  replacing glass doors, 21
  thermostats, 21

Tools, 11–13

U. L. knot 17–18, 52

Vacuum cleaners
  motor malfunctions, 32–33
  switch replacement, 33

Vibrators
  buzzer type, 30
  motor driven, 30–31

Volt-ohm-milliameter (VOM), 12–13